STUDIES IN GERMAN LITERATURE

Volume V

□ □

THE NACHTWACHEN VON BONAVENTURA

A STRUCTURAL INTERPRETATION

by

JEFFREY L. SAMMONS

1965

MOUTON & CO.

LONDON · THE HAGUE · PARIS

Printed in The Netherlands.

ACKNOWLEDGEMENTS

The present study is based upon my doctoral dissertation, "A Structural Analysis of the *Nachtwachen von Bonaventura*", presented to the Faculty of the Graduate School of Yale University in partial fulfillment of the requirements for the Ph.D. in May, 1962. I must here express my appreciation to Prof. Heinrich Henel, whose advice and patient encouragement were invaluable to me in the course of that labor.

Thanks are due to the libraries of the Universities of Hamburg, Freiburg, and Frankfurt am Main and to the State Library of the Czechoslovakian Soviet Socialist Republic for providing me with copies of unpublished dissertations. I am grateful to Prof. Cecil Wood of the University of Minnesota for his advice on statistical problems, and to Prof. Henry Kucera of Brown University, without whose generous and time-consuming assistance I should not have been able to manage those problems; Mr. George Monroe of Brown was also of assistance in these matters. Prof. Wolfgang Paulsen of the University of Connecticut put himself to constant trouble for me, and through continuous correspondence and several conversations made an inestimable contribution to the final version. Prof. Detlev Schumann of Brown very kindly read the original manuscript and offered many helpful suggestions. I owe gratitude to Miss Eva J. Schweizer of the City University of New York, who ran innumerable errands for me in New Haven and New York and assisted me in preparing the manuscript, and to Mr. Edgar F. Beckham of Wesleyan University for unrestricted permission to use an unpublished paper.

Providence, Rhode Island, April, 1964

TABLE OF CONTENTS

BIBLIOGRAPHICAL NOTE

All quotations of the *Nachtwachen* text are taken from the copy of the original edition now in the German Literature Collection of the Sterling Memorial Library at Yale University. The pagination of the original edition is reproduced in the editions of Hermann Michel (Berlin, 1904, where it is noted in the margin), Erich Frank (Heidelberg, 1912), and Raimund Steinert (Weimar, 1914, 1916, 1917, Potsdam, 1920). For the convenience of those not having access to these editions I shall also include, in Roman numerals, the number of the night-watch in which the quotation appears, then followed by the original page number.

I. THE STATE OF
NACHTWACHEN SCHOLARSHIP

In the year 1804[1] there appeared in the *Journal von neuen deutschen Original Romanen,* one of the numerous ill-fated periodicals of the Romantic era, a pseudonymous item entitled *Nachtwachen. Von Bonaventura.* The pseudonymity of the work, the generally indifferent character of the vehicle in which it appeared, and the obscurity of the place of publication (Penig in Saxony) all suggested a rather dim future for the book. In fact, it can be safely said that only one factor kept it from disappearing totally into the extra-canonical limbo of the world's literature, and that is that the work was originally ascribed to the Romantic philosopher F. W. J. Schelling. This ascription, though certainly incorrect, is by no means unreasonable on the face of it; in 1802 Schelling had indeed published two poems under the pseudonym "Bonaventura",[2] and Jean Paul himself assumed that Schelling was the author.[3] But the sole documentary evidence that Schelling might have produced the book rests on the rather shaky authority of Varnhagen von Ense,[4] and a gradual recognition of the clear discrepancy between the contents of the *Nachtwachen* and Schel-

---

[1] For the question of dating, see the first item of the bibliography at the end of this study.

[2] See *Nachtwachen von Bonaventura,* ed. Hermann Michel (Berlin, 1904), pp. xxxv-xxxviii, hereafter cited as Michel, *Nw;* Franz Schultz, *Der Verfasser der Nachtwachen von Bonaventura. Untersuchungen zur deutschen Romantik* (Berlin, 1909), pp. 3-147, hereafter cited as Schultz, *Verfasser.*

[3] Ernst Förster, *Denkwürdigkeiten aus dem Leben von Jean Paul Friedrich Richter* (Munich, 1863), I, 457; see also Schultz, *Verfasser,* pp. 31-32 and n. 3.

[4] Karl August Varnhagen von Ense, *Tagebücher* (Leipzig, 1861), II, 206.

ling's mentality eventually provided the leverage with which the work was recovered from obscurity. Thus it is only by virtue of a quite gratuitous accident that the *Nachtwachen* has entered our historical conciousness of German literature.

These facts determine the history of *Nachtwachen* scholarship, which I shall here review in order to explain more clearly the contribution which this study attempts to make. There is no evidence that the book made any stir whatsoever upon publication; it is not surprising that an omnivorous reader such as Jean Paul should have run across it, but otherwise it seems to have been totally unknown, at least among the opinion-makers, and unknown and forgotten it remained for decades. Not until 1877 did the first reprinted edition, under the editorship of Alfred Meissner, appear;[5] from Meissner's remarks in this edition and elsewhere,[6] one gathers that his interest in the matter derived partly from polemical considerations vis-à-vis Schelling. Schelling's connection with the *Nachtwachen* gradually, but with increasing momentum, became a subject of critical discussion,[7] and in 1903 the first alternative suggestion was made in Richard M. Meyer's proposal of E. T. A. Hoffmann as the author.[8] Two years later, Caroline Schlegel was also somewhat implausibly suggested.

[5] *Nachtwachen von Bonaventura*, ed. Alfred Meissner (= *Bibliothek deutscher Curiosa*, Vols. II-III) (Lindau and Leipzig, 1877; Berlin, 1881).

[6] Alfred Meissner, *Mosaik* (Berlin, 1886), II, 17-31. For an examination of Meissner's part in the controversy, see Schultz, *Verfasser*, pp. 60-67.

[7] E.g., Rudolf Seydel, "Schellings Nachtwachen", *Zeitschrift für deutsches Altertum*, XXIII (1879), 203-205; Erich Schmidt, "Nachtwachen von Bonaventura", *Vierteljahrschrift für Literaturgeschichte*, I (1888), 502.

[8] Richard M. Meyer, "Nachtwachen von Bonaventura", *Euphorion*, X (1903), 578-588. The Hoffmann theses was to some extent supported by Gottfried Thimme, "Nachtwachen von Bonaventura", *Euphorion*, XIII (1906), 159-184.

[9] Erich Eckertz, "Nachtwachen von Bonaventura", *Zeitschrift für Bücherfreunde*, IX (1905-06), 234-249. Josef Körner, in a note to his edition of *August Wilhelm und Friedrich Schlegel im Briefwechsel mit Schiller und Goethe* (Leipzig, 1926), p. 216, suggests, without giving any reasons, the Viennese journalist Johann Karl Christian Fischer as his candidate for the authorship. Although this hypothesis found its way into one edition of the *Großer Brockhaus*, sub "Bonaventura", III (Leipzig, 1929), 144; sub "Fischer, Johann Karl Christian", VI (Leipzig, 1930), 268, it has never been systematically argued in print. Körner's discussion of Fischer in "Die Wiener 'Friedensblätter' 1814-15, eine romantische Zeitschrift", *Zeitschrift*

Meanwhile it became apparent that Meissner's text was inadequate, not to mention his comments on it, and so in 1904 Hermann Michel produced first some opinions on the subject[10] and then a text, complete with introduction, notes and index, for the series *Deutsche Literaturdenkmale des 18. und 19. Jahrhunderts*.[11] Although Michel was unimpressed by Meyer's Hoffmann theory and expressed some lingering doubts about Schelling's authorship, the edition represented no advance in the study of this problem; its great virtue was the considerable amount of factual material it assembled, particularly with regard to parallels out of contemporary literature and expository writing. In the following year, in the course of a generally favorable review of Michel's work, Oskar Walzel objected that neither Michel nor anyone else had presented any critical analysis aimed at the text, and quite sensible suggested that a thoroughgoing literary interpretation ought to be the next step in coping with it.[12] This, however, was not to be for some time to come.

In 1909 came another new edition[13] accompanied by another study,[14] but this time of totally different quality, for now Franz Schultz devoted a volume of over three hundred pages to the question of the authorship of the *Nachtwachen*. There is a rather odd contradiction in this massive undertaking; Schultz asserts in his preface:

Wie anderen Literarhistorikern, die sich in neuerer Zeit mit schwierigen Verfasserfragen beschäftigten, wurde auch mir nicht die gesicherte Nennung des Autornamens das Wesentliche, sondern die Kennzeichnung des Geistes, der sich in dem mysteriösen Werk regt,[15]

---

für Bücherfreunde, n.s. XIV (1922), 95-96, does not mention the *Nachtwachen*.

[10] Hermann Michel, "Nachtwachen von Bonaventura", *Nationalzeitung*, Jan. 13, 15, 1804.

[11] Michel, *Nw.*

[12] Oskar Walzel, [review of Michel], *Deutsche Literaturzeitung*, XXVI (1905), cols. 2862-6; see also his "Schriften zur Romantik", *Das literarische Echo*, VIII (1905-06), cols. 574-575.

[13] *Nachtwachen von Bonaventura*, ed. Franz Schultz (Leipzig, 1909).

[14] Schultz, *Verfasser*.

[15] Schultz, *Verfasser*, p. v.

but in point of fact exactly the opposite is true. It becomes increasingly clear throughout the essay that Schultz is uninterested in and indeed contemptuous of the *Nachtwachen* as a literary work, and that he regards his study purely as an exhibition of proper methodology in scholarly questions of this kind. As a matter of fact, this concern reaches evangelistic proportions, leading Schultz to employ exceedingly intemperate language in speaking of those scholars and writers whose theories he is demolishing. But demolish them he does; with infinite patience and enormous industry he untangles the complex history of the ascription to Schelling and shows it to be baseless; he then proceeds to destroy the other hypotheses as well. On the positive side he presents a suggestion of his own: after accumulating a mass of external evidence and internal parallels, he comes to the conclusion that the most probable author is an all-but-forgotten writer, Friedrich Gottlob Wetzel (1779-1819).[16]

Schultz's argument in favor of Wetzel falls into three main parts. He begins by examining the *Journal von neuen deutschen Original Romanen* and finds there another anonymous novel, Nos. 3-4 of the series of 1804, *Die Kirche und die Götter,* which has been definitely assigned to Gotthilf Heinrich Schubert (1780-1860).[17] In discovering Wetzel in the circle of Schubert's close friends, Schultz shows that Wetzel had suitable connections with Dienemann's publishing house to make publication of a novel there plausible. Schultz then gathered together as many of Wetzel's works and unpublished letters as he could find; from these, as well as from autobiographical sources, it is clear that from about 1800

---

[16] This hypothesis in turn sparked a revival of interest in Wetzel, the most important fruit of which is Hans Trube, *Friedrich Gottlob Wetzels Leben und Werk mit besonderer Berücksichtigung seiner Lyrik* (= *Germanische Studien*, No. 58) (Berlin, 1928). Trube has little to say about the *Nachtwachen*. In assessing Wetzel it is useful to remember that Heine gave him a brief but admiring notice in *Die romantische Schule*; see Heinrich Heine, *Sämtliche Werke,* ed. Ernst Elster (Leipzig and Vienna, [1887-90]), V, 351.

[17] Schultz, *Verfasser,* pp. 178-179. Schubert himself admitted his authorship in his autobiography, *Der Erwerb aus einem vergangenen und die Erwartungen von einem zukünftigen Leben* (Erlangen, 1854-56), II, pt. 1, 73-79. Why this particular novel should be the logical starting point in the search for the author of the *Nachtwachen* is not clear.

to 1805 Wetzel anonymously published several novels in a desperate effort to keep body and soul together; some of these have never been identified.[18] Thus Schultz proves that the external evidence does not contradict the possibility that Wetzel could have written the *Nachtwachen,* since the work would then be among the number of otherwise unidentified items. For the third part of this argument, Schultz examines Wetzel's works and adduces a series of parallel passages which, he claims, demonstrate beyond any doubt that the *Nachtwachen* is from Wetzel's hand.

It is this third part of Schultz's presentation which is most difficult to assess critically. This is because we are not presented here with a single logical argument, but with a series of more or less weak links in a chain of proof in which the whole is presumed to be greater than the sum of the parts. To meet the argument successfully, therefore, it would be necessary to examine each parallel individually; it would be merely carping to select a few which are less than convincing and use them to discredit the entire presentation. Such an approach would be impractical not only because of the great number of parallels but also because they are arranged in a somewhat disorderly manner, without regard to type of parallelism or chronology within Wetzel's works. Some of the examples show verbal similarities while the point of the passage is quite different from or sometimes contradictory to the corresponding passage in the *Nachtwachen*; in other cases the theme is similar but the wording quite unlike. It must be said that there is a wide range between two extremes; some of the parallels are exceedingly tempting whereas others are utter nonsense. A considerable proportion of them share either conventions and commonplaces of the literary environment, or are echoes of particular literary figures, notably Jean Paul and Novalis.[19] The would-be critic of Schultz is placed in the impossible position of having to assess the merits of each individual instance in order somehow to draw a sum of probability from the whole. Nor is this

[18] Schultz, *Verfasser,* pp. 220-231.
[19] Schultz readily admits this, *Verfasser,* pp. 247-251, 256-259. Schultz calls attention to several more, but ignores others. For example, there is a clear dependence upon Lessing in the two passages compared on pp. 291-292 which refer to death as the brother of sleep.

the only problem; there are a number of others. The uncertainty of the purely hermeneutic approach to questions of authorship is amply demonstrated in areas where a great deal of energy and intelligence has been applied: Bible criticism, Homer, and the *Nibelungenlied,* not to mention the nearly dormant quarrel over the identity of Shakespeare. It is fair to say that in none of these cases, with the exception of the last, have there been anything like universally acceptable hypotheses.

When we leave the area of verbal parallels, and particularly of sentence rhythm, where Schultz's argument is at its strongest,[20] it is not easy to bring the atmosphere of the *Nachtwachen* into accord with what we otherwise know about Wetzel. Here, too, there are reasons why it is difficult to come to terms with Schultz's argument, because the materials he brings together are so widely distributed and some of them so difficult of access that no one has undertaken the task of retracing Schultz's steps in order to meet him on his own ground. Wetzel's works themselves are very difficult to come by.[21] From these we get an impression of un-

---

[20] See especially the impressive list of parallels at the end of Schultz's study, pp. 320-325.

[21] I have been able to see only a part of Wetzel's extensive corpus of writing. His play, *Hermannfried letzter König von Thüringien* (Berlin, 1818), is one of a series of standard historical dramas with strong patriotic and anti-French intent, and is in any case too late to be of any help to us here. Wetzel's major work in the period in question is *Magischer Spiegel* (1806); the only edition I have seen (ed. Kristian Kraus, Leipzig, 1939) is unfortunately worthless as a text because by the editor's own admission (pp. 21-23), it has been abridged, rewritten and "modernized", presumably for Nazi propaganda purposes. It is an intensely patriotic and idealistic work, cast in the form of a vision and in language imitative of Jakob Böhme, which prophesies the hegemony of the German spirit over the world. Through the courtesy of Prof. Wolfgang Paulsen of the University of Connecticut I have had an opportunity to examine 1) *F. G. Wetzel's gesammelte Gedichte und Nachlaß,* ed. Z. Funck (pseud. for Karl Friedrich Kunz, Leipzig, 1838), 2) *Schriftproben von F. G. Wetzel. Mythen – Romanzen – Lyrische Gedichte* (Bamberg, 1814), and 3) *Schriftproben von F. C. [sic] Wetzel. Zweytes Bändchen* (Bamberg and Leipzig, 1818), as well as Friedrich Engel, *Einige Briefe von Friedrich Gottlob Wetzel, herausgegeben und seinem Töchterchen Minna zum Tauftage gewidmet* (Leipzig, 1903). The contents of these poetry volumes, while they have precious little to do with the *Nachtwachen,* nevertheless reveal a substantial minor poet who undoubtedly will bear further study. In addition to the extensive selections given by Trube and Schultz, a number of poems and other

shakeable idealism finding its expression most clearly in nationalist sentiment, which gradually crystallized into the Prussian pan-German variety.[22] It would be impossible to read such attitudes out of the *Nachtwachen*. Furthermore, if the book is Wetzel's work, it falls in the period of his engagement to his dearly beloved fiancee, Johanna Heuäcker. Schultz argues that Wetzel's unsettled disposition during this period is congruent with the *Nachtwachen*,[23] but Trube, who is in no sense whatever an opponent of Schultz's hypothesis, about which he expresses no reservation,[24] and who made an intensive study of Wetzel's love-poetry in this period, has the following to say about the atmosphere it breathes: "Von der sicheren Basis dieses Glaubens [an Schellings Naturphilosophie] ist die kraftvolle Lebensbejahung, welche den Gedichten Wetzels wiederum eigen ist, zu verstehen".[25] That this statement could not even remotely be made of the *Nachtwachen* will become evident in the course of this study; the work exhibits precisely the opposite of "Lebensbejahung". One student has aptly characterized Wetzel when he speaks of his "wenig problematische Natur, seine trotz mancher Zweifel vorhandene Sicherheit im christlichen Glauben und in der romantischen Urgrund-Mystik".[26] Thus in the last analysis one is thrust back upon one's own intuition. By and large Schultz's results were received with approval by the scholarly world.[27] While Wetzel is generally named as the most probable

---

quotations appear in Z. Funck, *Erinnerungen aus meinem Leben in biographischen Denksteinen und anderen Mittheilungen*, Vol. I: *Aus dem Leben zweier Dichter: Ernst Theodor Wilhelm Hoffmann's und Friedrich Gottlob Wetzel's* (Leipzig, 1836), which is the primary source for biographical information about Wetzel.

[22] Trube, pp. 68-74.
[23] Schultz, *Verfasser*, p. 247.
[24] Trube, pp. 5-6.
[25] Trube, p. 155.
[26] Joachim Stachow, "Studien zu den Nachtwachen von Bonaventura mit besonderer Berücksichtigung des Marionettenproblems" (diss. Hamburg, [1959]), p. 36.
[27] Richard M. Meyer, [review of Schultz], *Euphorion*, XVI (1909), 797-800, is the most important admiring review, while quite justly complaining of the unnecessarily rude treatment Schultz accorded him in his book. An example of a cautiously negative attitude is found in the appendix to Rudolf Haller, *Die Romantik in der Zeit der Umkehr* (Bonn, 1941), pp. 262-263. Wilhelm Kosch's review in *Literarische Rundschau für das katho-*

author, with some notable exceptions to which I shall come presently, it has usually been customary to continue to regard the *Nachtwachen* as an anonymous work and to refrain from bringing Wetzel into the interpretive picture. I can only give it as my own opinion, unsupported by an exhaustive rebuttal of Schultz's study, that the Wetzel hypothesis is hard to believe; not only is everything of Wetzel's I have seen very different from the *Nachtwachen* in attitude, but also vastly inferior to it in diction and compression. Indeed, if Wetzel is to be elevated to a position of importance in the literature of his time, it must be chiefly on the basis of the *Nachtwachen*. In one respect, however, I am in a position to attack an assumption which is basic to Schultz's theory. He makes much of what he regards as technical carelessness and structural chaos in the *Nachtwachen*; it is because he finds such basic incompetence in Wetzel that he regards the latter as a likely candidate.[28] This basic assumption, which Schultz shares with other scholars, is flatly contradicted by the results of the present study.

Schultz did not succeed in closing the debate on the authorship of the *Nachtwachen,* for in 1912 a scholar named Erich Frank brought forth yet a third double contribution of a new edition and supplementary study.[29] We now find the work ascribed to none other than Clemens Brentano. In one respect Frank's method represents an advance over that of Schultz; he proposes to deal with the stylistic material as presented in the text, and to proceed from that base to a search for the author. Under "style" Frank subsumes a number of orthographic peculiarities, but the core of the argument consists in an observation concerning the extraordinary frequency of the optional dative -*e*-ending in strong masculine and neuter monosyllables, which is a stylistic device insofar as it reflects qualities of sentence rhythm. Frank finds that

---

lische Deutschland, XXXVII (1911), cols. 502-504, is exceedingly skeptical of Schultz's method.

[28] Schultz, *Verfasser,* pp. 263-264.

[29] *Clemens Brentano. Nachtwachen von Bonaventura,* ed. Frank (Heidelberg, 1912), hereafter cited as Frank, *Nw*; Frank, "Clemens Brentano, Nachtwachen von Bonaventura", *Germanisch-Romanische Monatsschrift,* IV (1912), 417-440. The introduction to the edition is an expanded version of the article.

on the average, of those words where the ending can appear, 96%
do have it in the *Nachtwachen,* a figure of some significance.
After performing a similar count in the works of twenty-two
writers of the eighteenth and nineteenth centuries,[30] he finds that
of the possible candidates for authorship, only Brentano shows
a comparable frequency (93-95%, as compared with Wetzel,
ranging in various works from 38 to 62%).[31] The rest of Frank's
argument exhibits embarrassing similarities to that of Schultz.
Brentano, like Wetzel, had connections with the publisher: Sophie
Mereau's translation of the *Spanische und italienische Novellen,*
done in collaboration with Brentano, appeared as No. 1 in the
1804 series of Dienemann's *Journal.* As in the case of Wetzel,
there is nothing in the external evidence to make Brentano's
authorship impossible; in his letters of the period he mentions a
number of plans which did not come to fruition in any known
work, some aspects of which have a vague connection with the
Nachtwachen. Finally, to complete the analogy, Frank presents a
set of parallel passages, which, like Schultz's, range from the
frivolous to the tempting, and which are subject to the same
objections as those raised in that connection. A careful reading
of Frank's study shows that the argument stands or falls on the
issue of the dative *-e-*ending, and here there are two problems.
First of all, it cannot be established to what extent the predilections
of the printer might be responsible for such an idiosyncrasy, since
we have no manuscript. Secondly, Frank's figures do not stand
unchallenged; Eduard Berend recounted the Brentano text and

---

[30] See the table in *Germanisch-Romanische Monatsschrift,* IV (1912),
434. To count Lessing (97%), Kant (56%), and Herder's *Ursprung der
Sprache* (64%) would seem irrelevant from a chronological point of view.
Even in a quarter of a century, particularly in a period of accelerated
literary development, such a feature might be subject to considerable varia-
tions.

[31] This wide range in Wetzel is in itself sufficient to cast doubt upon
the reliability of the method. The figures are: *Kleon* (1802), 62%; *Fischers
Reise* (1805), 42%; *Browns Briefe* (1806), 38%. Thus the frequency has
dropped by nearly half within four years. Brentano's *Godwi,* which shows
the highest frequency in those works counted by Frank (95%), is separated
from the *Nachtwachen,* as near as we can tell, by some three years. To
what extent is similarity significant if it can show such wide variation in
the works of a single author?

found a much lower frequency.[32] Frank's study was roundly condemned by the reviewers,[33] and with that, the Brentano hypothesis passed out of the main stream of *Nachtwachen* scholarship. It was, however, by no means dead, as we shall now see.

The Brentano hypothesis reappeared again in a brief but somewhat comical interlude when Friedrich Gundolf reasserted it as an opinion without presenting much in the way of argumentation.[34] This touched off a retort from the old master himself,[35] who excoriated Gundolf not only for his position on the *Nachtwachen*, but also for his responsibility for what Schultz regarded as a new school of literary criticism which had abandoned the painstaking procedures of solid scholarship. Thus Schultz used the *Nachtwachen* again as he had previously, as an object of model procedure in philology. Apparently Gundolf was properly impressed, for he dropped the argument when he reprinted the essay two years later.[36]

At this point there is a break in the chain of scholarship. Although the scholars might quarrel with one another as to conclusions, at each stage they were familiar with all the preceding work on the subject. In 1921, however, a dissertation was presented to the University of Prague by one Karl Hofmann,[37] which has been completely ignored by all subsequent students. This is not because the existence of the dissertation was unknown – it appears

---

[32] *Euphorion*, XIX (1912), 796-813.

[33] In addition to Berend's, the other reviews, all negative, are: Heinz Amelung, "Neues und Altes, Echtes und Falsches von Clemens Brentano", *Das literarische Echo*, XV (1912-13), cols. 1114-9; H. Cardaunus, "Wer war Bonaventura?", *Hochland*, X (1912-13), 751-754; Friedrich Schulze, [review of Frank], *Literarisches Zentralblatt*, LXV (1914), cols. 554-555; Max Morris, [review of Frank], *Deutsche Rundschau*, CLIV (1913), 474; Schultz, "Zu den 'Nachtwachen von Bonaventura'", *Archiv für das Studium der neueren Sprachen und Literaturen*, CXXIX (1912), 12-15. Schultz replied by adducing a set of particularly weak additional parallels with Wetzel.

[34] Friedrich Gundolf, "Über Clemens Brentano", *Zeitschrift für Deutschkunde*, XII (1928), 1-17; 97-115, esp. p. 12.

[35] Franz Schultz, "Gundolf und die Nachtwachen von Bonaventura", *Euphorion*, XXIX (1928), 234-239.

[36] Gundolf, *Romantiker* (Berlin, 1930), pp. 277-336.

[37] "Zur Verfasserfrage der Nachtwachen von Bonaventura" (diss. Prague [1921]).

regularly in bibliographies of *Nachtwachen* materials – but perhaps because it exists only in manuscript (it is written in a relatively clear *Fraktur*). The dissertation, however, is an interesting attempt to put the question of authorship on a new and more reliable basis. Hofmann criticizes both Schultz and Frank not only for their method of adducing parallels, but also on the ground that their approach is *a priori*: a candidate for authorship is selected and then all possible evidence is collected which might support the claim with varying degrees of cogency. Hofmann quite rightly points out that the only evidence we have is the text itself, and he proposes to extract from this text reliable materials for making comparisons. His method consists in a statistical examination of certain elements of style.[38] The theory underlying the method is that there are certain types of words which lie below the conscious level of stylistic formation. They are the "little" words – in the case of Hofmann's study, conjunctions, particles and adverbs.[39] It is clear that Hofmann is tending towards a definition of what

[38] Hofmann derives his methodology from the following studies: Constantin Ritter, "Die Sprachstatistik in Anwendung auf Goethes Prosa", *Euphorion,* X (1903), 558-578; Ritter, "Die Sprachstatistik in Anwendung auf Platon und Goethe", *Neue Jahrbücher für das klassische Altertum Geschichte und deutsche Literatur,* XI (1903), 241-261; 313-325; Ritter, "Anwendung der Sprach-Statistik auf die Recensionen in den Frankfurter gelehrten Anzeigen von 1772", *Goethe-Jahrbuch,* XXIV (1903), 185-203; Max Morris, *Goethes und Herders Anteil an dem Jahrgang 1772 der Frankfurter gelehrten Anzeigen* (Stuttgart, 1909); Hans von Arnim, *Sprachliche Forschungen zur Chronologie der Platonischen Dialoge* (= *Sitzungsberichte der Kaiserlichen Akademie der Wissenschaften in Wien,* Philosophische-Historische Klasse, CLXIX, Abhandlung 3) (Vienna, 1912); Kurt Gassen, *Die Chronologie der Novellen Heinrich von Kleists* (= *Forschungen zur neueren Literaturgeschichte,* Vol. LV) (Weimar, 1920).

[39] Hofmann is not aware of the difficulties attendant upon the class "adverb" when applied to German. He does not distinguish between adverbials (those words and phrases which function always and only as adverbs, which, from a syntactical point of view, includes also prepositional phrases), and adjective-adverbs, whose function is differentiated only by the presence or absence of inflection, raising the question whether it is not formally more useful to identify adjectives in predicate position as adverbs. Since Hofmann is concerned with elements which are not determined by content, it would not seem reasonable to distinguish between adjective-adverbs in adjectival and in adverbial position, since both have an equal measure of lexical meaning. Some problems raised by this consideration will appear below.

are today called "function words", that is, those words whose syntactic function predominates over lexical meaning, and which cannot be replaced, as "content words" can, without altering the basic sentence structure. It is further assumed that the relative frequency of such subconscious stylistic elements differs from author to author and, in the works of the same author, changes over the course of time. If these assumptions are correct, it ought to be possible, given sufficient text, to identify an unknown author if other works of his are extant, or, as the case may be, establish a chronology of the works of the same author, by comparing the relative frequency of subliminal stylistic elements. To this end, Hofmann has counted the conjunctions, particles, and adverbs in the *Nachtwachen.* Because he considers, on the basis of the external evidence presented by Frank, the Brentano hypothesis to be the most probable, he begins his search by making a similar count of a section of equal length (approximately 39,000 words) of that work of Brentano's which is closest in time to the *Nacht-wachen, Godwi* (1801), leaving out, of course, the lyric passages.[40] As a result, Hofmann comes to two conclusions: first, that the *Nachtwachen* as a whole is stylistically compatible with Brentano's *Godwi,* and second, that the *Nachtwachen* text is not itself a unity, but that Chapters I, II, V, XI and part of X differ so radically from the remainder that they must be by another hand.[41] Hofmann then launches himself upon a tortuous argument based upon parallel passages, a procedure for which he seriously criticizes Schultz and Frank, and concludes that the work was written by Brentano, with the incompatible chapters supplied by his fiancee, Sophie Mereau.

---

[40] Hofmann fails to identify the edition he counted, but from the page numbers given, it is apparent that it is *Clemens Brentanos Sämtliche Werke,* ed. Carl Schüddekopf, et al., V (Munich and Leipzig, 1909), 215-300, 401-471.

[41] Hofmann's inspiration for this idea derives from the report that when the *Nachtwachen* was subjected to Sievers' famous "Schallanalyse", Sievers expressed the opinion that the work was not a unity (Hofmann, pp. 102-105). Sievers' "test" is reported by Friedrich Schulze, *Literarisches Zentralblatt,* LV (1914), cols. 554-555. It need hardly be pointed out that Sievers' opinion is worthless as scholarship, since the method cannot be communicated.

Assuming that Hofmann's count is correct, his selection of words suitable, and his method pertinent, the first question to ask is whether the statistics he presents do in fact support his claim. To determine this, I performed a rough chi-square test for statistical compatibility on Hofmann's frequency lists. The chi-square test is a mathematical procedure for discovering, within certain predetermined limits of probability, whether the deviations of observed frequency in two populations can be explained in terms of random chance distribution.[42] If the result falls within the limits of chi-square, the frequency deviations in the two populations (in this case, the two texts) may be due to chance; if the value is significantly greater than chi-square, the hypothesis that the populations are homogenous is not proven. It is important to note the limitations of proof involved: in the first instance, the result does not necessarily prove that the populations *are* homogenous; in the second instance, the result does not necessarily prove that the texts *cannot* be by the same hand. The same limitations, incidentally apply to Hofmann's method as a whole.

When applied to Hofmann's first assertion, that the *Nachtwachen* and *Godwi* are statistically compatible, the results of the test not only fail to bear him out, but are so wildly out of line as to reduce the argument to nonsense. This result derives chiefly from the following inconvenient fact: in the *Nachtwachen* Hofmann has counted a total of 459 lexical items for a total of 6,070 words, and in the text of equal length from *Godwi,* 374 lexical items for a total of 4,974 words. It will be seen that not only is the total of lexical items in the classes counted much larger in the *Nachtwachen,* but also the proportion of words in these classes to the whole text is significantly larger in the *Nachtwachen* than in *Godwi.* It is therefore not possible to get results even approaching statistical significance for the list as a whole, and indeed the very fact that the *Nachtwachen* lexicon in these classes is so much larger should be grounds for suspicion. To point out certain

[42] The chi-square test for good fit was applied essentially as described by Sidney F. Mack, *Elementary Statistics* (New York, 1960), pp. 134-139. Sincere thanks are due to Prof. Henry Kucera of Brown University, who cheerfully gave of his valuable time to help me set up this problem correctly.

individual frequencies in the lists which show more or less "close-ness', such as the accidental fact that *dieser* (conjunction, particle, or adverb?) occurs in each text 212 times, is of no statistical significance.[43] The results of the test, when applied to Hofmann's second assertion, are slightly more favorable to him, though not by much. Here he is trying to demonstrate the opposite, namely that Chapters I, II, V, XI, and part of X are *not* stylistically compatible with the remainder. To support this claim, Hofmann extracts from his list fifty-five words which he claims demonstrate the difference between the two parts. When the chi-square test is performed on this list, the result is the same as in the first case: the value is well beyond the limit of statistical compatibility, though to be sure not by the huge margin as in the first test; however, it is *non-compatibility* which Hofmann is trying to demonstrate.[44] How-

[43] For those familiar with the chi-square test, the following details may be of interest. The problem is complicated not only by the fact that there are so many more terms with zero-frequency in the *Godwi* text than in the *Nachtwachen,* but also because the text counted is so short, with the result that the majority of the terms show total frequencies of less than five. Since it is a rule-of-thumb in the chi-square test that no cell should be smaller than five, it was necessary to combine these small cells into larger ones, thus further beclouding the issue of the selection of parameters. After various attempts at combination I finally produced a list with 110 terms. The value of chi-square for 110 terms (assuming 109 degrees of freedom) with 95% probability is 133.98. The total for the list was 3,077.12. This figure is so large that it could not be made to suggest significance even if the assumed probability were substantially lowered, which would, in any case, further vitiate the validity of the claim. It should also be observed that since there is no external control in the form of a standard frequency list for German in the first decade of the nineteenth century, the *Godwi* text was itself used as the "expected" frequency, since it is claimed that the *Nachtwachen* conforms to it. This further distorts the result, for in those cases where the *Godwi* frequency was greater than that in the *Nachtwachen,* the resulting value for that term was appreciably smaller than for an equal deviation in the other direction. This is evident from the formula by which the chi-square value is derived, $\frac{(o-e)^2}{e}$ where o is the observed frequency in the *Nachtwachen* and e, in this case, the frequency in *Godwi.*

[44] The same difficulties with respect to zero-frequencies and small cells apply also to this list; after combining, I produced a list with 47 terms (46 degrees of freedom). The expected frequency was computed differently, however. For purposes of setting up the test it was assumed that the text *is* homogenous, and further, that such an assumption implies normal dis-

ever, after removing seven adjective-adverbs from the list, which, contrary to Hofmann's theory, have lexical and not structural force, the results are still beyond the limits of good fit, but by a very small margin.[45] Thus the statistical evidence, when subjected to a reliable mathematical test, tends to contradict directly the conclusions which Hofmann draws from it.

Having satisfactorily disposed of the substance of Hofmann's argument, we can now turn to some general considerations. There are a number of intrinsic problems in his method. First of all, the 39,000-word text of the *Nachtwachen* is very short for any kind of statistical analysis; frequencies occur which are too small for significance. Second is the lack of an adequate control; we do not have, and are not likely to get, a normative German word-frequency list for the period in question. Thus it is impossible to get a completely reliable measure of expected frequency. These deficiencies can be remedied somewhat only by counting much more text: a Brentano text several times the length of the *Nachtwachen,* as well as an appreciable amount of Wetzel; as a substitute for the nonexistent control, it would be useful also to count one or more texts which do not bear on the authorship problem at all; for example, Goethe's *Wahlverwandschaften* (1809). Furthermore, if the method of examining presumably subliminal elements of style is to be pursued, then a more accurate definition of function words is needed, along with perhaps a refined typology of clause and phrase structure. In addition to better linguistic techniques, the dictates of common sense should not be forgotten. For example, Hofmann includes the word *nichts* in his list. Under most circumstances, one could perhaps argue that the word has little enough

---

tribution of lexical items throughout the text. Thus the total text was taken to give the expected frequency. Since text a (I, II, V, XI, and part of X) stands to text b (the remainder) in a ratio of approximately 1 : 4.5, the expected frequency for the text a is given by the formula $\frac{2}{11}$ (a + b). The value of chi-square for 46 degrees of freedom is 62.7; the total for the list, 96.83.

[45] The value of chi-square for 40 terms (39 degrees of freedom) with 95% probability is 54.1. The total for the revised list is 59.00. In this case it is permissible to edit the list, since Hofmann himself extracted it from the total list.

lexical force to be considered a function word. In this text, however, that is not the case; the word *nichts* is utterly central to the
thematic impact of the *Nachtwachen,* and thus cannot be counted
in a list of subconscious stylistic elements. It happens to be one of
those words which contribute to the lopsidedness of the statistical
comparison, for it occurs sixty-nine times in the *Nachtwachen* and
by some curious chance, not at all in the sections of *Godwi* which
were counted.[46] The same stricture applies to such judgments as
Hofmann's claim that the work falls into two stylistically incompatible parts. One does not need a statistical analysis to demonstrate, for example, that Chapter V differs stylistically from the
main body of the work. This is precisely what this chapter is
meant to do; it retells, as an ordinary prose narrative, the story
presented in a quite different way in the preceding chapter.[47] The
watchman is quite clear about this: "Da konnte ich nun nichts
bessers thun, als mir meine poetisch tolle Nacht in klare langweilige Prosa übersetzen, und ich brachte das Leben des Wahnsinnigen recht motivirt und vernünftig zu Papiere" (V, 78-79).
Moreover, the idyll in Chapter XI contrasts specifically in form
and content with the general tone of the book, and the same thing
can be said, in a more subtle sense, of I and II. What is needed
here is not statistics, but an intelligent reading of the work with a
willingness to account for its structural arrangement. In this connection it is useful to bear in mind the inherent limitations of the
statistical method. Though useful results may well be obtained by
a word-frequency study properly set up (this is why one must
regret that Hofmann's study remained unknown, since it might
have been followed up with more convincing work), stylo-statistics

---

[46] As in the case of *dieser,* it is by no means clear why *nichts* is in-
cluded in the list of conjunctions, particles, and adverbs. *Nichts* is none of
these things, but from a syntactical point of view clearly a substantive.
Even odder is the fact that *nicht,* which can be satisfactorily regarded as
adverbial in most contexts, if indeed not in all, does not occur in Hofmann's list, except as a component of phrases.

[47] Hofmann speculates that Sophie Mereau rewrote the story in IV in
order to fill up pages (p. 126). This is undoubtedly the worst single interpretation to be found anywhere in *Nachtwachen* studies. What I hope may
be regarded as a more credible treatment of this feature of the book will
be found in the following chapter.

cannot be made to bear the whole burden of proof. If the frequencies in two texts turn out to be statistically compatible, this proves only that they *can* be by the same hand, not necessarily that they *are,* especially when an adequate normative control is lacking. Conversely, if the frequencies are beyond the limit of compatibility, it is by no means proven that they cannot be by the same hand, due to the assumptions involved. It is assumed, for example, that in a relatively short text one may expect something approaching a normal distribution of particular lexical items, which is by no means certain, and it is further assumed that the items selected are actually below the level of conscious stylistic will, which is even less certain, especially in cases where it can be shown that the narrative is purposefully of a different type. As has been remarked apropos of Bible criticism, such methods could easily be employed to prove that Macaulay could not have written both his history of England and the penal code of India.[48]

---

[48] Despite the logical and methodological difficulties inherent in comparisons of this kind, another effort has been made recently to shed some light on the matter by statistical methods: J. Thiele, "Untersuchungen zur Frage des Autors der 'Nachtwachen von Bonaventura' mit Hilfe einfacher Textcharakteristiken", *Grundlagenstudien aus Kybernetik und Geisteswissenschaft,* IV (1963), 36-44. Here texts from Schelling, Brentano (*Godwi*) and Wetzel (*Kleon,* 1802) are compared with sections of the *Nachtwachen* text. Thiele avoids the difficulties arising from low frequencies when counting individual words by comparing median sentence length, median number of syllables per word and median length of chains of words with an equal number of syllables; all of these points are sensibly taken because they bear on subliminal syntactical rhythm, especially the third. It is not surprising that the Schelling texts, which are of a philosophical nature, should vary greatly from the others with respect to points one and two. For the rest, Thiele computes that the Wetzel text substantially agrees with the *Nachtwachen* text, whereas Brentano's text varies significantly from both. Thus his conclusion: "von den hier geprüften Autoren [käme] nur Wezel [sic] als möglicher Verfasser der 'Nachtwachen' in Betracht" (p. 37). Although Thiele has done work which, in contrast to Hofmann's, may be statistically significant (Prof. Henry Kučera and Mr. George Monroe of Brown University have expressed to me some doubts about this), he is still laboring under the same questionable assumptions, namely, "dass zur gleichen Zeit verfasste Arbeiten eines Autors, die der gleichen Literaturgattung zuzurechnen sind, im Durchschnitt der einzelnen Abschnitte gleiche Textkonstanten aufweisen" (p. 36; cf. n. 36 above; furthermore, the Schelling texts are pointless within the terms of this assumption), and that an *a priori* selection of candidates from among the known Romantics can

After this, the issue of the *Nachtwachen* lay dormant for fifteen years. It is true that writers of literary histories and special studies found themselves increasingly obliged to take note of it as a representative phenomenon of the Romantic period,[49] and it appeared in the series *Deutsche Literatur in Entwicklungsreihen*,[50] but although Walzel in 1905 had called for an individual interpretation of the work, nothing of the kind was attempted until 1936, when Joachim Müller devoted an essay of moderate length to the subject.[51] This study is a thoughtful exposition of the spirit that speaks out of the *Nachtwachen*, but it could by no means be called a close reading of the text, and for that reason some of Müller's judgments fail to stand up under analysis.[52] Nearly twenty more years were to go by before a new stage of investigation, a stage of careful textual analysis, was to begin.

Three dissertations open the new era. The first of them, Sigrid Gölz, "Die Formen der Unmittelbarkeit in den Nachtwachen von Bonaventura" (diss., Frankfurt am Main [1955]), attempts to place the *Nachtwachen* at the transition point between the older, or Jena, Romanticism, and the younger, or Heidelberg, variety. To do this the author discusses the way in which Bonaventura deals with the forms of "Unmittelbarkeit", that is, those realms in which

---

turn up the author with any degree of probability. Thus the matter can be said to stand exactly where it stood before.

[49] E.g., Josef Nadler, *Literaturgeschichte der deutschen Stämme und Landschaften*, III, 2d edn. (Regensburg, 1924), 384; Eleonore Rapp, *Die Marionette in der deutschen Dichtung vom Sturm und Drang bis zur Romantik* (Leipzig, 1924), passim; Richard Majut, *Lebensbühne und Marionette. Ein Beitrag zur seelengeschichtlichen Entwicklung von der Genie-Zeit bis zum Biedermeier* (= *Germanische Studien*, No. 100) (Berlin, 1931), pp. 28-34.

[50] "Reihe Romantik", XVI, ed. Andreas Müller (Leipzig, 1930), 13-117; notes on pp. 246-251.

[51] Joachim Müller, "Die Nachtwachen von Bonaventura", *Neue Jahrbücher für Wissenschaft und Jugendbildung*, XII (1936), 433-444.

[52] So as not to leave this statement unsupported, I shall give one example. Müller says of the watchman's love affair in the madhouse, "Als er schon im Begriff ist, das 'Narrenkämmerchen' als Lebensbereich anzusehen, 'eine Narrenpropaganda und eine ausgebreitete Kolonie von Verrückten' zu errichten, wagt er den Schritt in die Wirklichkeit der Liebe" (*ibid.*, p. 439); the text (XIV, 233), however, makes it clear that this plan is a *result* of his growing love for Ophelia.

the older Romantics tried to put themselves into direct spiritual contact with the soul of the universe (i.e., love, art, childhood, nature), and which the younger Romantics found so ambivalent. She concludes that the abandonment of selfhood, of finite contact in favor of communion with the infinite, which these forms of "Unmittelbarkeit" required, led not to the expected harmony and ecstasy, but to demonic terror and spiritual displacement, and she finds Bonaventura's treatment of precisely these themes to be symptomatic of this transition.

This study was followed a year later by Heinrich Köster, "Das Phänomen des Lächerlichen in der Dichtung um 1800 (Jean Paul, E. T. A. Hoffmann, Bonaventura)" (diss. Freiburg im Breisgau, [1956]). The author concludes that while for Jean Paul laughter serves to overcome the painfully felt discrepancy between the ideal and the real, in Hoffmann and even more in Bonaventura it begins to represent the only possible true response to *all* perception. Thus Bonaventura in particular represents the essential untenability of the Romantic view of life and the world.

The third in the series of dissertations, Joachim Stachow, "Studien zu den Nachtwachen von Bonaventura mit besonderer Berücksichtigung des Marionettenproblems" (diss., Hamburg, [1957]), opens with a sharp critique of the authorship problem as it now stands; Stachow particularly points out, with some justice, that the effect of Schultz's treatment is to turn Wetzel into a Bonaventura-type personality, which does violence to the real nature of Wetzel's works.[53] For his own part, Stachow clearly asserts, "daß die Werkdeutung nicht als letztes Ziel angestrebt wurde. Die Werkdeutung sollte vielmehr die Erkenntnis geschichtlicher Strukturzusammenhänge vorbereiten, die als das eigentliche Ziel bezeichnet werden muß".[54] He then develops a detailed examination of the qualities of irony in the *Nachtwachen,* particularly as they reflect the principles of Friedrich Schlegel, and of the marionette-motif and the motifs related to it, both as symbolically significant in themselves and as determinants of style. The study closes with shorter examinations of nature description, the

[53] Stachow, pp. 35-36.
[54] Stachow, p. 44.

concept of love and the critique of art. Although Stachow disclaims interpretation of the work as such as his ultimate purpose, it is in fact in just this area that he achieves a significant advance beyond the earlier studies discussed here: he is prepared to take the composition of the *Nachtwachen* more seriously than his predecessors. He speaks of an attempt, "die Verflochtenheit der Werkkomponenten in den Blick zu bekommen",[55] and comes to the important conclusion that the work "verläuft in merkwürdigem Hin-und-Her von gleichsam milderen zu radikalen Positionen, die kontrastierend aneinandergefügt sind".[56] Despite this insight, which might perhaps have been more fruitful had Stachow confined himself to interpretation, he is in the end unable to find a real rationale in the composition. Like others before him, he finds the *Nachtwachen* to be arbitrarily ordered, and, like the others, is unable to fasten upon it clearly as an independent work of art.

Following upon these three dissertations there appeared a full-length monograph on the subject, Dorothee Sölle-Nipperdey's *Untersuchung zur Struktur der Nachtwachen von Bonaventura.*[57] A brief examination of this important study will be necessary in order to define the differences between her approach and mine. What is meant here by "Struktur" is inner structure, that is, patterns of narration and the form of the world which the author creates. The elements of the work are analyzed from various points of view; there is a division into retrospective biographical report, present night-watch report and present event; a discussion of the relationship of the narrator to the material and to his audience, and an analysis of the narrative perspective. The narrative procedures are divided into such categories as reportage, description, judgment, and reflection, providing a clear presentation of the meaningful functions of these various techniques. The epic patterns are arranged under such headings as conversation, scene, vignette, oratory, monologue, etc., and the structure of

---

[55] *Ibid.*

[56] Stachow, p. 47.

[57] Palaestra, No. 230 (Göttingen, 1959), hereafter cited as Sölle-Nipperdey. This is a revised version of her Göttingen dissertation of 1954, submitted under the same title.

space and time are discussed with the conclusion that the epic
space created in the *Nachtwachen* is nothingness and time the
infinitude of boredom. Thus the view of "Struktur" in this study
is difficult and complex:

Die bloße Angabe oder Formel der Struktur ist hier, anders als etwa
in der Chemie, unzureichend, nein falsch, weil sie den intentionalen,
d.h. den bedeutungsvoll verweisenden Charakter nicht deutlich machen kann. Die Intentionalität der Struktur ist nichts anderes als
Existenzauslegung, die sich im Kunstwerk vollzieht und jeweils ein
bestimmtes Verständnis von dem Dasein des Menschen in der Welt
offenbart.[58]

Though this point of view leads to some plausible and enlightening
results about the quality of form in the work, it may fairly be
asked whether the structure "intends" "Existenzauslegung" rather
than perhaps some such thing as "Existenzdarlegung". In any
case, though Sölle-Nipperdey make use of highly sophisticated
interpretative techniques, I myself am in doubt as to whether
these techniques are not used as an exercise in the identification of
literary devices and typologies rather than as instruments in the
specific analysis of this particular work; in other words, whether
the work is not the object rather than the subject of her study.
There remains still undone an effort to describe and interpret the
Nachtwachen as a self-contained, consistently formed work of art.
It is this task to which I have set myself.

The term "structure" also appears in the title of the present
study, and consequently I am obliged to explain in what sense I
use the word. My view of structure for the purposes of this essay
is simple and elemental: it is "construction"; it denotes the way
in which the pieces of the work are put together. This aspect of
the matter Sölle-Nipperdey calls "Aufbau", and she subordinates
it to the larger issue of "Struktur".[59] It may appear to be something of a retrogression to move from the sophisticated concept of
"Struktur" in Sölle-Nipperdey to the relatively naive view of
"structure" in this study. But I believe it is a useful rule of literary
criticism to proceed from the elementary to the profound in

[58] Sölle-Nipperdey, p. 9.
[59] Sölle-Nipperdey, p. 11.

organized fashion; we must know what the work *is* before we can say what it *means*. Now this issue is particularly pertinent to the *Nachtwachen* because there is a consensus of opinion on the subject of "Aufbau" running from Michel through Schultz to Sölle-Nipperdey,[60] and it is essentially this: the materials presented in the *Nachtwachen* are a chaotic, uncontrolled potpourri; the author has written down anything that came into his head in the order in which it occurred to him, and the division into night-watches, their order and indeed their number is a matter of chance and not of artistic intent. Now if this is in fact true, Sölle-Nipperdey's study can stand as written, but if it is not true, some basic revision of attitude toward the work is required. I assert that it is not true, and that there is in fact artistic meaning in the external form of the *Nachtwachen*. This thesis, involving a re-examination of the "Aufbau", is at the base of the present study. I shall begin with an analysis of the order of night-watches and the pattern which I believe they form, and then proceed to a discussion of the watchman's own development of attitude and its implications for this method of ordering, and thirdly to details of the manner in which the attitudes of the watchman are structurally presented. Finally, I shall try to connect the *Nachtwachen* in some measure with the literary atmosphere in which it appeared, including detailed comparisons with other pertinent works, and I shall append what is an attempt at the first exhaustive bibliography of materials relative to the *Nachtwachen*. By doing this I hope to open a new perspective of appreciation for the artistic quality of this curious and still imperfectly understood work.

---

[60] Michel, *Nw*, p. xvii; Schultz, *Verfasser*, pp. 125-126; Sölle-Nipperdey, p. 13.

II. THE SEQUENCE OF THE SIXTEEN
NIGHT-WATCHES

1. A superficial glance at the *Nachtwachen* as a whole reveals the fact that the work is divided into sixteen night-watches. This must now be our starting point, because if an analysis of the external structure by the method I have mentioned is possible at all, we must somehow be able to make sense out of the order of the night-watches. This is particularly the case because the work is a fictional biography told entirely out of chronological order, and it is just this apparently arbitrary rearrangement of materials which invites our curiosity. The basis outlines of the watchman's biography are these: he was conceived on Christmas Eve by a gypsy woman; his father was an alchemist who had succeeded in exorcising the devil, and the latter stood godfather to the child (center portion of XVI); the gypsy buried the boy in a casket in the earth and directed a shoemaker to find him, enabling the watchman to grow up as a shoemaker-poet in the tradition of Jakob Böhme and Hans Sachs (first part of IV); he acquires a certain reputation as a poet, but his behavior at a trial for satirical slander lands him in the madhouse (VII); his stay there (IX) leads to a love affair with another inmate who dies in childbirth (XIV); he is expelled from the madhouse and becomes a marionetteer, but the troupe is broken up as politically dangerous, so he obtains a post as a night-watchman (XV). In this post he is deprived of his horn and prohibited from singing for announcing the Day of Judgment (VI); he becomes involved in a quarrel between a dying atheist and the Church (I, II, and part of III), he interferes with and prevents an adulterous tryst (III), he listens to the life story of an unhappy, mad Spaniard (latter part of IV), and retells the

story in a different style (V); he recounts the suicide of an un-successful author (VIII), is present as a nun is buried alive for having given birth to a child (X) and tells the life story of the child's father (XI); endeavors to prevent a suicide, which turns out to be merely play-acting (XII), pays a visit to an art museum with appropriate satirical comments (XIII), and finally enters a cemetery where he learns of his ancestry and opens his father's grave (remainder of XVI).

Thus the true chronological order of the night-watches is as follows: XVI, IV, VII, IX, XIV, XV, VI, I, II, III, (IV), V, VIII, X, XI, XII, XIII, (XVI). It seems that it is this apparently helter-skelter arrangement which has convinced the critics that the work was written without plan or form. To be sure, there are definite chronological difficulties. The original impression of the reader that he is accompanying the watchman on his rounds can-not be sustained. Night-watch X clearly takes place on a winter night in which a beggar freezes to death, while the first sentence of XIII places the action at the vernal equinox. Thus the effect of successive night-watches, which we have clearly in I, II, and III, is not maintained. More serious is the frequently observed problem of the watchman's horn; in II he uses his horn as an "antipoeticum" (13-14), and in III he blows his horn as part of his intervention in the adulterous situation (35), but in VI he relates how he lost the right to blow the horn altogether (109-110). One solution to this problem would be to abandon any attempt to regard I, II, and III as related in the present, and to place VI chronologically between III and IV. Equally possible, however, is that it is merely a slip on the part of the author, which one need not erect into a theory of technical incompetence, for such mistakes in detail appear in the works of the most careful of writers. In any case, however, any attempt to resolve this anomaly as an irony of the author would lead away from the nature of the work: Bonaventura does not play with his materials simply to exhibit his artistic sovereignty. Furthermore, we cannot regard all the night-watches as having taken place previous to the narration, for it seems necessary to regard the final chapter as subsequent to the telling of the earlier biographical events, in which the watchman gives no evidence of being aware of his ancestry. In the satirical speculation concerning his descent from the devil and "einer eben kanonisirten Heiligen" (VII, 112), one gets the impression that at this point in his narrative the watchman is ignorant of his family background.

In the face of such evidence of carelessness, is it possible also to find evidence that the *Nachtwachen* is indeed a planned and organized work? Those of us whose profession it is to read literary works over and over again until we are as sure as we can be of the character of their content do well to remember that fiction is after all essentially a linear art; that is, a work is presumably written to be read from front to back, once. It will be useful to ask if any indication of organization appears to the reader upon such a first reading. Despite the numerous assertions of all critics to the contrary, it seems to me that there are at least two such indications. The first is the juxtaposition of IV and V wherein the same story is told twice. Schultz's remark, that

das erste Capriccio hat assoziativ das zweite hervorgerufen: der Autor schreibt eben ohne Zucht und Selbstbeherrschung frischweg nieder, was ihm in den Sinn kommt,[1]

seems to me to indicate an utter unwillingness to consider what the import of such a striking device might be. On the contrary, this juxtaposition fairly demands interpretation within the context of the work, and thus is an indication of organizational intent. A second such indication is the tension created between IX and XIV. Night-watch IX begins:

Es freut mich daß ich in den vielen Dornen meines Lebens doch wenigsten Eine blühende volle Rose fand; sie war zwar so von den Stacheln umschlungen, daß ich sie nur mit blutiger Hand und entblättert hervorziehen konnte; doch aber pflükte ich sie, und ihr sterbender Duft that mir wohl. Diesen einen Wonnemonat unter den übrigen Winter- und Herbstmonden verlebte ich – im Tollhause. (IX, 153)

The chapter ends: "Für meinen Wonnemonat im Tollhause spare ich ein anderes Nachtstück auf" (IX, 173). The importance of the event to which this remark points, the love affair in XIV, will be

---

[1] Schultz, *Verfasser,* p. 126.

discussed at length below. It is sufficient to note here that Bonaventura is aware, as he writes IX, of what will take place later.
Thus we are able to see that the author has the plan of the work
more or less clearly in mind. He does not set down in random
order the first thing that occurs to him. As we look at the work
more closely, we are able to find other evidence of the author's
awareness of the structure as a whole. In the first night-watch he
refers briefly to his own career as a poet (I, 3-4), which is however not described until VII. Similarly, in II he remarks, "und
doch war ich Poet, Bänkelsänger, Marionettendirekteur und alles
dergleichen Geistreiches nach einander" (16), which points ahead
not only to the contents of VII but also of XV. The gypsy woman
who appears on the woodcut in IV (45) indicates the author's
awareness of the watchman's antecedents as they are to be
revealed in XVI. The stranger who appears in X is mentioned
only with these words: "Plötzlich stieß ich auf jemand in Mantel
– was ich von ihm erfuhr, gehört in die folgende Winternacht;
was ich that, noch in diese" (X, 182), and indeed, his story is
told in XI. From all this the suspicion grows that we have in fact
a planned, thought-out narrative and not a random *jeu d'esprit*;
these passages far outweigh the evidence of carelessness noted
above. The critics who deny this have, I fear, not themselves tried
their hand at constructing a consistent fictional narrative.

With all this evidence in hand, we are obliged once again to
look at the work as a whole, this time in the order in which it is
presented to us. At the risk of redundancy we must again describe
the content of the night-watches, because both the chronological
rearrangement and the wealth of detail make it imperative that
the contents of the work be kept clearly in mind in the course
of the discussion which follows.

Under threatening night skies the watchman introduces us to
the town poet, who works at night in order to escape his creditors,
and to a dying atheist surrounded by his grieving family as well as
to a frustrated priest who roars threats of hell-fire and damnation
into the dying man's ears. This situation develops into a scene of
grisly slapstick as priests disguised as devils endeavor to kidnap
the body; they are foiled by the dead man's brother, and the

Church exploits popular superstition in order to cover up the situation. Shortly thereafter the watchman foils a pair of adulterers, delivering them with heavy irony into the hands of the dry, bloodless husband. Then the watchman meets a Spaniard whose unhappy love affair has led him to a terrible crime, but for years he has inexplicably been prevented from taking his own life. The story is told twice, first by the Spaniard in the form of a marionette play with the characters of the *Commedia dell' Arte,* and then again by the watchman in sober prose (I-V).

Next the watchman tells the story of the commotion he caused by announcing the Day of Judgment on the last night of the century; he then reaches into his own past and describes how his satirical writings and ballads landed him first in prison and then in the madhouse; following this he recounts the suicide of the town poet, who hangs himself upon receipt of his rejected tragedy (VI-VIII).

Now the watchman returns again to satire, describing the inmates of the madhouse, including one who believes himself to be God the Creator; following this is a chapter containing three vignettes: in quick succession we see a beggar freezing to death, the wedding of a young man at the same time as the funeral of his abandoned love, and a violently misanthropic porter who directs the watchman to the burial of an Ursuline who has given birth to a child. The watchman then tells part of the story of the father of that child (IX-XI).

A fourth time the watchman turns to satire, describing a character who prides himself on acquiring the external trappings of great men, and narrating his own blunder in attempting to dissuade an actor who as merely practising a suicide scene. This is followed by a "Dithryrambus über den Frühling" and a visit to an art museum, in which the statues seem to come to life in a bitter phantasy. Then comes the great and gripping chapter which describes his own love affair in the madhouse (XII-XIV). He reaches again into his past to describe his career as a marionetteer, and closes the work with the scene in the cemetery, where he meets his mother and watches the remains of his father dissolve into nothingness (XV-XVI).

My purpose in retelling the story in this fashion has been to show what I believe is structurally the case in this work; that it is basically cyclical in nature. Obviously this cyclical structure is neither completely symmetrical nor rigidly consistent, but nonetheless it appears that we have the same type of progression repeated five times: a beginning which is essentially satirical, frequently abounding in commentary, based on materials either out of the watchman's past or from the night-watches themselves; this satirical display then gradually leads into a situation which is catastrophic in character, in which the satirical elements yield to an increasing nihilism and a muted or repressed despair, and the comedy to an acrid and barely relieved bitterness. These five catastrophes – the Spaniard's tale of love and crime, the suicide of the poet, the young man whose beloved is buried alive, the tragic end of the watchman's moment of happiness in the madhouse, and the final outburst of total nihilism in the cemetery – are the points of demarcation for the structure of the *Nachtwachen.* Each time the catastrophe is told, it is as though the author had taken a breath, and we find ourselves once again in the relatively harmless realm of satire, as the process begins anew, but each time we are increasingly in the shadow of the preceding horror; the satire becomes less occasional and more existential in impact, the comedy more hollow, until finally the responses of the reader are crushed under the increasing weight of nihilism and he is able to comprehend the outburst in the concluding chapter. This is basically the external structure of the *Nachtwachen,* and it will be useful to look in detail at each of the five sections which I have postulated.

2. If we return again to our method of inquiring after the impression left by a first reading, certainly it would seem reasonable to find the reader in a state of bewilderment after having perused I-V. Perhaps the impression given by this section taken alone, a first impression, of course, accounts for the insistence of critics upon the disorganized quality of the work, for it is only when seen from the perspective of the work as a whole that the motifs of this section fall into place. We are introduced to the town

poet in I and II, and he is apostrophized in I by the watchman,
yet he appears here only as the stimulus for satirical and bitter
observations and does not become a central figure until VIII.
Nor are we really aware of the depth of bitterness in the watchman's remarks until more of the fabric of his soul has been
unfolded for us. Upon a first reading, such a remark as:

Ich bannte diesen poetischen Teufel in mir, der am Ende immer nur
schadenfroh über meine Schwäche aufzulachen pflegte, gewöhnlich
durch das Beschwörungsmittel der Musik. Jezt pflege ich nur ein
paarmal gellend ins Horn zu stoßen, und da geht's auch vorüber
(II,13)

is greeted with amusement; we admire the cleverness of his "antipoeticum". In the course of time the matter takes on a darker cast.

As for the phantasmagoria surrounding the death of the atheist,
it requires a certain amount of attention on the part of the reader
to make out just what is going on. But when we have untangled
the mystifications, the devilish priests masquerading as devils, and
the compounded embarrassment of the Church, which, in order
to avoid identification of the dead priest, claps his severed head
into a locked reliquary and thus inadvertently gives rise to the
dangerous belief that the devil has been killed, we believe we have
merely extravagant comedy at the expense of the Church. We have
not yet seen enough of the ubiquitous motif of the mask, the
Larve, to be aware of the implications of the scene.

Our bafflement grows when faced with the extended anecdote
of frustrated adultery. Not only does the scene appear to have
nothing whatever to do with the foregoing, but in addition irony
is piled upon irony so that it is difficult to say just what is being
satirized. Basic to the situation is the ancient motif of adultery
behind the back of a deserving cuckold,

ein Wesen . . ., von dem ich anfangs zweifelhaft blieb, ob es ein
Mensch oder eine mechanische Figur sey, so sehr war alles Menschliche an ihm verwischt, und nur bloß der Ausdruck von Arbeit ge-
blieben. (III, 30-31)

But the watchman is by no means a partisan of the adulterous pair:

Der Mann ließ es sich recht angelegen sein im rhetorischen Bom-

bast, und sprach in einem Athem von Liebe und Treue; das Frauen-
bild dagegen zweifelte gläubig, und machte viel künstlichen Hände-
ringens (III,29);

these are characters under the spell of the fashionable literature
so despised by the watchman: the wife speaks in the jargon of
popular Romanticism, and the lover has "die Moral völlig, dem
Geiste der neuesten Theorien gemäß, abgewiesen" (III, 32-33,
35). The watchman interferes in this miserable triangle by delivering the couple to the mercies of the unworthy husband, thus serving
a morality to which one might have thought him in opposition,
considering his admiration of the atheist in I and II. Added to
this is the opening section of IV, where the watchman in relatively
warm and sentimental tones tells us something about his childhood in a style quite different from the frenetic satire which
precedes. And to top off the confusion, we then have a story
which is told twice.

Before turning to that problem, it is important to assert now
that this confusion is only apparent. In fact, the night-watches
I-V serve as an introduction to the whole work, and it is not an
exaggeration to say that the whole *Gehalt* of the *Nachtwachen* is
contained, one way or another, in these chapters, a fact which,
however, can only be appreciated once the entire work has been
assimilated. Bonaventura's deep disgust with the literary and
intellectual climate of his age, exhibited here in the three anecdotes
described above, pervades the work, and it is only its existential
quality which has not yet been made clear. We shall see eventually
that both the story of the atheist and the ironies of the anecdote
of adultery are indicative of the total decay of values which the
work finally asserts. The two most pervasive motifs of the *Nachtwachen,* the mask and the marionette, are introduced in their
characteristic context in these chapters. The way in which these
matters are subsequently developed will be the subject of later
sections of this study. It is sufficient here to assert that they are
contained in embryo in this first cycle.

The story which is told twice is that of a Spanish gentleman
who falls in love with an unknown lady, but while he is searching
for her, his brother marries her. The disappointed lover then

arranges for his brother to kill his wife and her page out of jealousy, and then to take his own life. Filled with bitter remorse, he perpetually endeavors to commit suicide, but is restrained by some unidentifiable force. In IV, this tale is told as a marionette play, in which the wooden lack of free will of the characters is described and the place of fate taken by Hanswurst, whose blundering prevents the gentleman from pursuing his love: "Jener will ihr nachstürzen, rennt aber, weil der Marionettendirektor hier ein Versehen macht, sehr hart gegen den Hanswurst" (IV, 65). His inability to take his own life is also ascribed to a clumsiness on the part of the director:

dann greift er, ohne ein Wort weiter zu sagen, ebenfalls nach dem Degen, um auch sich selbst, zu guter lezt, hinterherzusenden; doch in diesem Augenblicke reißt der Drath, den der Direktor zu starr anzieht, und der Arm kann den Stoß nicht vollführen und hängt unbeweglich nieder. (IV, 71)

There is a distinct satirical element in this passage; whether or not the marionette play is a satire on Schiller's *Braut von Messina,* as has been both asserted[2] and denied,[3] is difficult to decide, but surely the contemporary theater is under the lash here. The import of the marionette itself is traditionally satirical, and the author of the *Nachtwachen* gives the motif additional force:

Für "Bonaventura" liegt der formale Wert des Marionettenstils vor allem in dem *Gegensatz* der unheimlich mechanischen Gebundenheit zu dem kühnen Willen und dem ins Unendliche strebenden Geist des Menschen, die jedes menschliche Wollen und Handeln anmaßend und nichtig, alles sittliche Streben lächerlich erscheinen läßt. Im Gewande des Marionettenspiels wird die Tragik des Lebens zur Posse, über die man sich "totlachen" kann, und zugleich zur beißenden Satire, gegen deren Bosheit niemand etwas einwenden darf, weil sie, scheinbar absichtslos, in der holzschnittartigen Primitivität und Steifheit selbst liegt.[4]

All this is certainly true, but it fails to take into consideration the

    [2] Richard M. Meyer, "Nachtwachen von Bonaventura", *Euphorion*, X (1903), 583.
    [3] Michel, *Nw*, pp. xxxii-xxxiii; Schultz, *Verfasser*, p. 161.
    [4] Eleonore Rapp, *Die Marionette in der deutschen Dichtung vom Sturm und Drang bis zur Romantik* (Leipzig, 1924), p. 38.

really striking aspect of the matter, the juxtaposition of this chapter with retelling of the story in the following night-watch. This time the watchman tells the story during the day, as a cure for insomnia:

Da konnte ich nun nichts bessers thun, als mir meine poetisch tolle Nacht in klare langweilige Prosa übersetzen, und ich brachte das Leben des Wahnsinnigen recht motivirt und vernünftig zu Papiere, und ließ es zur Lust und Ergözlichkeit der gescheuten Tagwandler abdrucken. (V, 78-79)

This he does in a manner which has no parallel elsewhere in the work, as has been noted by Sölle-Nipperdey:

Demgegenüber ist nun die zweite Fassung die ausgedehnteste Einheit von Bericht, die in den *Nachtwachen* überhaupt vorkommt. Hier wird in einer völlig anderen Sprache gesprochen wie sonst in den *Nachtwachen*. Der Rhythmus drängt vorwärts, die rhythmischen Kola sind länger als üblich und stellen so den schroffsten Gegensatz zu der abgehackten, steifen, trockenen Sprache des Marionettenspielers dar.[5]

The characters now have names; the Spanish setting is clearly presented; Don Juan's emotional responses, such as his feelings upon seeing Ines for the first time (V, 83), are described in detail, psychological observations are made (*ibid.*), the tale is complicated by the growth of an unspoken love between Don Juan and Ines (V, 86-87), etc. For a moment we are tempted to say that the story, first told satirically and bitterly from the perspective of Don Juan's madness, is here given psychological depth and realistic coloring. But soon we realize that this cannot be; not only does it make no structural sense in the work as a whole, but we have seen that the watchman himself speaks of the second narration with the utmost contempt. We are driven to argue that the second narration is in fact inferior to the first, that the psychology presented is not a deeper insight but a superficial explanation for an action that is in actual fact wooden, cold, and not subject to free will, that emotions are not real but simply painted on and built in, and that the director of life (i.e., God), is an incompetent fumbler. Why then is the tale told twice?

[5] Sölle-Nipperdey, pp. 34-35.

Whatever the conscious intention of the author might have been, surely this juxtaposition serves as a graphic elucidation of Bonaventura's method. For it underlines the fact that he is not writing phantasy, and at bottom he is not writing satire. Every aspect of the work is a reflection of a reality such as is presented in V, but a reality stripped of its illusion and deception, cleaned of emotion, meaning and the delusion of free will, such as is presented in IV. The story told in IV is truer than the same story told in V, and this is the kind of truth, extracted from the outward appearance of the world as a whole, which will pervade the entire work. There is no need for further explanation, no need to re-translate the subsequent narration "so recht zusammenhängend und schlechtweg . . ., wie andre ehrliche protestantische Dichter und Zeitschriftsteller" (VI, 93); it has been done once, and the method, when seen against the background of the whole work, becomes abundantly clear. Seen from this standpoint, it is evident that the juxtaposition of IV and V properly belongs in the introductory section, indeed, rounds it off as a unity.

3. When we leave the unsettling implications of IV and V, we find ourselves in the somewhat more breathable atmosphere of satire in VI. There is great comedy in the Day of Judgment hoax which the watchman creates out of pure whimsy, comedy directed against both the hypocrisy of society and the gullibility of the towspeople. From the point of view of external structure there is little to be said about this chapter. But it must be kept in mind that the satire of VI stands in the shadow of what we have learned from the first cycle. The very universality of the satire, directed against king, nobility, jurists, clergymen, and the whole range of society, gives us pause, for who escapes the reckoning? Only the town poet, the watchman's alter ego in the garret, and a man whose satirical curiosity transcends the pretended earnestness of the moment, so that he takes his own life to see if it is still possible in the last moments of Creation.

In VII we pick up a strand of biography which was begun in IV. A brief comparison of these two passages will be useful here; more will be said about the watchman's biographical development in the next chapter. In IV, using as a fiction a book of woodcuts which describe his life,[6] he draws vignettes out of his childhood as the shoemaker's foundling, emphasizing especially his interest in Böhme and Hans Sachs, and he describes the shoemaker's astonishment at the boy's gifts and open-hearted response to nature. In VII this idyll of childhood is left behind, as the boy's poetic gifts and peculiarity of viewpoint lead him into frustration. His "Leichenrede" upon the birth of a child, dilating upon the physical fact that the human being begins to die as soon as he is born, is misunderstood and used as a funeral eulogy. A general satire upon the necessity of asses in the world is taken personally by a citizen,[7] and the young man lands in prison. He fares no better in his subsequent career as a *Bänkelsänger*; his satirical ballads bring libel suits upon him. His defense in court is an attack upon the morality of judges in general, and the bewildered judges see no other recourse than to have the young man committed to the madhouse. So ends his poetic career.

The following night-watch describes the end of another career, that of the local author already mentioned in I, II, and VI. The connection with the preceding night-watch is clear enough, for it is just such an end that the watchman has escaped by abandoning his poetic vocation. Already in I he has observed:

Aber ich habe diese Beschäftigung [die Dichtung] aufgegeben gegen ein ehrliches Handwerk, das seinen Mann ernährt.... Nachtwächter sind wir zwar beide; schade nur daß dir deine Nachtwachen in dieser kalt prosaischen Zeit nichts einbringen, indeß die meinigen doch immer ein Uebriges abwerfen. Als ich noch in der Nacht poesirte, wie du, mußte ich hungern, wie du, und sang tauben Ohren; das letzte thue ich zwar noch jetzt, aber man bezahlt mich dafür. O Freund Poet, wer jezt leben will, der darf nicht dichten! (I, 3-4)

The bitterness which is caused by this capitulation and symbolized by the horn used to repress "diesen poetischen Teufel in mir"

---

[6] One is rather reminded of the book of life in the fifth chapter of Novalis' *Heinrich von Ofterdingen*.

[7] This personage is identified in the text by three asterisks. Frank, *Nw*, p. xc, calls attention to the fact that Fichte was sometimes alluded to in this manner, and thus identifies this fleeting figure with Fichte. This seems quite far-fetched to me.

(II, 13) is sufficiently clear. But the poet, though he belongs "zu den Idealisten, die man mit Gewalt durch Hunger, Gläubiger, Gerichtsfrohne u.s.w. zu Realisten bekehrt hatte" (VIII, 131), remains true to his vocation, despite starvation, and concentrates on a tragedy entitled *Der Mensch* which will demask the world and reveal it for what it is. The tragedy is rejected, and the poet hangs himself with the string from the package in which it is returned. There is no real differentiation in style or content between that which the poet is supposed to have written and the watchman's own mode of expression. The poet is in a very real sense the watchman's alter ego; he has remained with the career with which the watchman began, and represents the end to which the watchman would necessarily have come had he not given up poetry.

Here a second section of the work closes naturally. We have begun with a general satire exposing the world as a whole; we have recapitulated the watchman's own poetic career and its violent collapse and then, by way of both of commentary and of deepening the unhappy significance of both presentations, we are witness to the miserable end of a poet who has combined an attempt to pursue his career with a realization of the shattering insights presented in VI. It is perhaps here more than at any other point in the work that we are tempted to agree with Josef Nadler that the *Nachtwachen* is by no means a Romantic book;[8] for the watchman's abdication from Parnassus and the implication that poetry is impossible in the world he describes, rather runs counter to the Romantic faith in the permanent and real value of poetry in the total existence of man. On the other hand, we will come to see, as a modification of this view, that the values of poetry have some permanence in the context of the work.

4. The ninth night-watch begins and ends with a reference to the most important single event in the watchman's life, his love affair in the madhouse, but, true to the pattern of the work which we have identified, this most shattering of all his experiences is

---

[8] *Literaturgeschichte der deutschen Stämme und Landschaften*, III, 2d edn. (Regensburg, 1924), 384.

postponed to XIV. Here we are back in the realm of satire again, as the various inmates are enumerated and described. The chapter is a kind of *Narrenschiff* in reverse; the fools, instead of being flayed themselves, are used as a stick with which to beat the world, for it is the unreasonableness of the world which has brought most of them to this pass.

Here it is worth saying that IX is unquestionably the weakest chapter in the book. The satirical possibilities of describing a set of twenty inmates of a madhouse are limitless, but Bonaventura's ordinarily rich imagination is simply not up to it. Of the nineteen inmates excluding the watchman, Nos. 1, 7, and 8 are also shipwrecked poets, while No. 5 is an orator whose speeches were too sensible and comprehensible. This preoccupation with the problem of the *Literat* in a work of universal satire is a bit parochial. Nos. 12, 13, 14, and 15 "sind Variazionen über denselben Gassenhauer, die Liebe" (IX, 168), without any effort to characterize them even briefly. No. 18, who pursues the mathematical impossibility of finding a final number, may be a reference to a contemporary personage, but if so, it has escaped the attention of the editors, and means nothing to the uninformed reader. The remark made upon No. 17, who concentrates upon his own nose: "Vertiefen sich doch oft ganze Fakultäten über einen einzigen Buchstaben, ob sie ihn für ein α oder ω nehmen sollen" (IX, 169), is insipid wit. If the continued accusations of the critics that Bonaventura is careless and lacks the will to artistic perfection have any validity, it is here in this night-watch.

On the positive side is the monologue of the Creator, who holds a ball in his hand as a symbol of the world and discourses regretfully upon the use man has made of Creation. The spark of the divine which he put in mankind was a mistake, and now he is at a loss as to what to do: "Am besten ich warte überhaupt mit der Entscheidung bis es mir einfällt einen jüngsten Tag festzusetzen und mir ein klügerer Gedanke beikommt –" (IX, 164). We have already been introduced, by implication, to the blundering God, in the person of the director of the marionette play in IV. Here we see essentially the same view from the perspective of God, rather than of man: the God who has spoiled his Creation by his own poor management expresses his contempt for the worthlessness and baseless intellectual pride of mankind. For the author the situation is a delicious vehicle for satire.

We must take note of the fact, however, that all the while the ground for satire has been sliding out from under our feet. For it is expected of the satirist that he have a fairly firm footing upon his own ideal, or, put in another way, he makes fun of imperfect superficial aspects of a world which is sound at the core, aspects which can be corrected by bringing them back into harmony with the ideal. Bonaventura himself is aware of this, for he begins VIII with a comment on the subject:

Bösartig aber werden sie [die Dichter] sobald sie sich erdreisten ihr Ideal an die Wirklichkeit zu halten, und nun in diese, mit der sie gar nichts zu schaffen haben sollten, zornig hineinschlagen. . . . Für den Maasstab ihres Ideals muß alles zu klein ausfallen, denn dieser reicht über die Wolken hinaus und sie selbst können sein Ende nicht absehen, und müssen sich nur an die Sterne als provisorische Grenzpunkte halten. (VIII, 130-131)

A satirical view of jurists presupposes a firmly held attitude toward justice; of adulterers, toward morality; of theologians, toward a proper religious attitude, etc. But in the course of the work this ideal ground begins to dissolve in the acid of the watchman's existential observations. Justice has no meaning if free will is denied, as it has been in IV; morality and religion have no base if God is an incompetent and fumbler who does not even know his own mind, as appears in IX. Gradually, with each succeeding cycle, the satire which opens the cycle becomes increasingly abysmal. These points will be discussed at length in a subsequent chapter. It is important to keep them in mind, however, while we are discussing the progression of the work. Furthermore, we will see immediately that the realm of satire is abandoned sooner in this section than in the two preceding, for the events of the next two night-watches throw an increasing pall of horror over these chapters.

The tenth night-watch contains three causally unconnected anecdotes told in succession. Again Schultz, who probably studied the *Nachtwachen* as thoroughly as anyone ever has, is appalled at the author's apparent lack of artistic discipline:

Wir erkennen bereits an diesem Ausschnitt die atomistische Art seines Denkens, die leichte Erregbarkeit seiner zerrissenen, immer vibrierenden Seele, die in den Gedanken und Gefühlen anderer sich selbst wiederfindet, die Unfähigkeit, seine absichtlich aufs höchste getriebene Eigenwilligkeit zu zügeln und der Leichtigkeit seines Schaffens regulierende Gewichte anzuhängen. Wir empfangen einen Vorgeschmack seiner zerfahrenen Technik, seiner hastenden, sprung-haften, improvisatorischen, skizzenhaften Darstellungs- und Aus-drucksweise.[9]

I confess to being baffled by this response. How is it possible for the careful reader not to observe that all three anecdotes turn upon the same dichotomy of love and death?

The first anecdote concerns a beggar who fights off slumber to keep from freezing to death in the cold night. The watchman considers whether or not to wake him, and finally consigns him to death. This is not the first shock of its kind in the *Nachtwachen* – the suicide in the Day of Judgment scene (VI, 98), which is directly the result of the watchman's prank, is another – but it is the most powerful. I do not know of a single parallel to this scene in the literature of the time, in Germany or out, and I believe one would have to go far into the nineteenth century before finding a comparable example of such programmatic cal-lousness. The horror is compounded in the accusation which the watchman makes against Death after the event:

O mörderischer Tod, der Bettler hatte noch eine Erinnerung an das Leben und die Liebe – die braune Locke seines Weibes hier unter den Lumpen auf der Brust; du hättest ihn nicht würgen sollen, – und doch —. (X, 177)

This leads to a monologue asserting that it is only the dream of love and the longing for it which has value, an idea which is picked up again under a somewhat different aspect in XVI.

The second anecdote describes a wedding which takes place in the same house as a funeral; the dead girl, "die weiße Braut", who has died of a broken heart after being abandoned by the

[9] Schultz, *Verfasser*, p. 95.

groom, is contrasted with the successful bride, "eine rothe Rose" (X, 179). It has long been recognized that both the motifs and the situation are in the ballad tradition;[10] there is in fact a specific reference to Bürger's "Lenore". But the importance of the brief phantasy lies in the juxtaposition of love and death again, with the hint that the dead girl has had the more fortunate experience.

Once these matters have been dealt with, we enter upon a situation which carries over into the next night-watch. The porter of an Ursuline cloister directs the watchman to a pageant of horror, in which a nun is buried alive as a punishment for having given birth to a child. This porter, we will come to see, is to some extent another alter ego of the watchman. A thoroughgoing misanthropist, he displays his dismay at mankind by putting his bitter questions to a bird which has been taught to respond with the one word "Mensch". In the face of the scene itself, in which the solemn pomp of the ceremony, the intimated quiet ecstasy of the victim, and the nocturnal, Gothic setting underline the horror of the situation, the watchman responds with a frenetic "Lauf durch die Skala" (X, 186-188). The events here described have created a pressure of terror which brings even the watchman to the edge of madness.

The eleventh night-watch serves as background explanation of the foregoing. It contains the tiny *Novelle* of a blind boy whose sight is restored by a miracle of medicine. In his sightless world he has become attached to a foster sister who sings to him; in a fierce twist of irony, however, the mother vows to give her adopted daughter to the Church if by some miracle the boy's sight should be restored. The short chapter ends in a gripping description of the boy's first experience of sight, which quite overwhelms him: "O Nacht, Nacht, kehre zurük! Ich ertrage all das Licht und die Liebe nicht länger!" (XI, 200).

It is a commonplace to remark that one of the supreme literary arts is the art of omission, the art of knowing what to leave out, thus preparing for the reader himself the joy or shock of discovery. That XI is a pure, one might even say, textbook example of this literary device, ought to be almost too obvious to mention.

---

[10]   E.g., Michel, *Nw*, p. xliv.

Yet even this chapter, in my opinion one of the strongest in the work, has been used as evidence for the putative incompetence of the author: it is asserted that the author lacked the artistic patience to finish the story![11] This is a result of an over-serious view of the opening remarks of XII (which of course again returns to the realm of satire), where the author puckishly states:

Es geht nun einmal höchst unregelmäßig in der Welt zu, deshalb unterbreche ich den Unbekannten im Mantel hier mitten in seiner Erzählung. . . . So gebe ich nach romantischen Stoffen hungernden Autoren mein Wort, daß sich ein mäßiges Honorar mit seinem Leben erschreiben ließe – sie mögen ihn nur aufsuchen und seine Geschichte beenden lassen. (XII, 201-202)

This is of course only an intended mystification which serves to draw the reader's attention to the artistic skill displayed in XI. We are easily able to supply the remainder: after the boy's sight is regained, his love for the girl who sang to him deepens, but his mother must carry out her vow to make her a nun. The young man pursues his love affair behind the walls of the cloister, and the result is the tragic scene described in X. To have told this story, some elements of which are fairly common coin in the literature of the period, would have been banal; to leave it to the reader's imagination seems to me to indicate a fine sense of structure on the part of the author. Here, as in the first cycle, we are given as a final chapter explanatory background after the significant aspect of the situation has been described.

Actually with the exception of the description of boyhood in IV (with which XI has certain affinities), there is no other passage in the *Nachtwachen* which displays more warmth, human compassion and even sentimentality than this night-watch. But just like the psychologically motivated tale in V, it is all basically illusion and delusion, for this sweet story of love and a medical miracle ends in frustration, death, and nameless horror. In order that we should be in no doubt on this point, the frustration, death,

---

[11] Frank, *Nw*, p. xxxix. Perhaps because it is so obvious, the interesting relationship of XI to X has not been explored in the secondary literature. There can be no doubt, however, that Schultz (*Verfasser*, pp. 194-195) seriously misunderstood the transition from X to XI.

and nameless horror are described to us *first*. We have come to
the end of another cycle.

5. By now we know what to expect on the heels of the foregoing:
a renewed burst of satire, and this is what we get in XII. The
terrible tales which have just been told have by no means obviated
the possibility for pure comedy, for we now meet a character who
could have come from the pen of Heine himself. This creature,
having discovered that he has "Kants Nase, Göthens Augen, Les-
sings Stirn, Schillers Mund und den Hintern mehrerer berühmter
Männer" (XII, 204), has managed also to acquire Kant's shoes,
Goethe's hat, Lessing's wig and Schiller's nightcap, in which outfit
he entertains society by weeping like Kotzebue and sneezing like
Tieck; and someone has informed him that his imitation of
Goethe's walk "amüsire ihn mehr, als Göthens neueste Schriften"
(XII, 205). The whole scene is a clever slap at the imitative,
popular authors of the time; only perhaps its point is somewhat
blunted for us by our recognition that Bonaventura's own work has
clearly derivative aspects, and perhaps there is some self-irony
involved, for it is just such self-irony which is the next order of
business.

There is something basically impertinent about true satire, for
it implies the attitude that the world is a pack of fools and only
the satirist himself has the right attitude toward things. But we
have already observed the fact, which we will have occasion later
on to discuss at length, that Bonaventura's satire lacks a solid
base of positive conviction. Under these circumstances, is it
possible that the satirical watchman should himself escape the
lash? Not if the author is writing a consistently structured work.
And indeed, it is now the watchman's turn to be the victim of
delusion. For now he comes upon an apparent suicide attempt;
to dissuade this gentleman, the watchman delivers an "Apologie
des Lebens" (XII, 208-214), which itself is a thinly-veiled re-
hearsal of the meaninglessness of human life. But the supposed
suicide is only a practicing actor attempting to work himself into
a "mäßiges Rasen" (XII, 214; a magnificently significant oxy-
moron), and for once the watchman himself has been gulled. The

ironies of this passage are inextricably intertwined. The apparent suicide scene is in a sense fake, but so is the burden of the watchman's "Apologie des Lebens", which is in fact just the opposite of what it claims to be, and although this double deception calls forth from the watchman an even more violent diatribe against the fraudulence of the world, the situation on which it is based is at bottom totally insignificant, for, after all, why should not the actor improve his skill in this fashion? In a sense the limits of satire have been reached at this point; the satire has turned upon itself, and the satirist himself has been caught in the web of it.

The chapter which follows is the most difficult in the entire book. It falls clearly into two parts: a "Dithyrambus über den Frühling", and a scene in a small art museum. From the structural point of view, problems abound in this chapter, some of which do not admit of a clear solution. Although we have been accustomed to think of the night-watches as taking place in the frozen stillness of winter, XIII describes "die Tag- und Nachtgleiche des Frühlings" (XIII, 217). The "Dithyrambus" itself, however, presents no insuperable difficulties; we are in the atmosphere of the Creator's monologue of IX and the misanthropic observations of the porter in X. The book of nature can be read joyfully until we come to man himself, who seems to contradict the logic of nature: "Kannst du es nimmer lösen, warum alle deine Geschöpfe träumend glücklich sind, und nur der Mensch wachend dasteht und fragend – ohne Antwort zu erhalten?" (XIII, 219).[12] Thus this passage fits into the pattern which has been taking shape in the *Nachtwachen* thus far. The scene in the museum immediately thereafter is more complex. It begins as follows: a dilettante climbs upon the pedestal of a Venus di Medici, "mit gespiztem Munde und fast thränend, um, wie es schien, ihr den Hintern, als den bekanntlich gelungensten Kunsttheil dieser Göttin, zu küssen" (XIII, 222). It is evident that on one level the watchman is busy grinding his satirical axes; he blasts the impiety of the modern age and its supercilious view toward the remnants of a

[12] Sölle-Nipperdey, p. 73, here calls attention to Jean Paul's motto for *Die unsichtbare Loge*: "Der Mensch ist der große Gedankenstrich im Buche der Natur."

more harmonious past. But the satire is by now totally integrated with more fundamental problems. Although for the most part interpretations are postponed to subsequent sections of this study, it is impossible to proceed here without making some effort to say what this scene means. There is a curious parallel between the use of the word "Göttertorso" here (XIII, 222; "Torso", XIII, 223) and the word "Naturtorso" (X, 175) occurring in the cold wintry night in which the beggar freezes to death. Of that night the watchman says: "Der kalte Tod steht in ihr" (*ibid.*); it is a night in which life has been amputated from nature, as it were. The statues of the gods have undergone amputation also; many of their limbs are missing, so that they are the wreckage of a piety which has long since lost its relevance. The modern age, by resurrecting these remnants of a lost relevance, has committed an absurd sacrilege, represented symbolically by the incapacity of modern experts to restore the missing limbs in any convincing manner (XIII, 223), and conceptually by the modern substitution of intellectual analysis for naive religious devotion: ". . . unsere moderne Kunstreligion betet in Kritiken, und hat die Andacht im Kopfe, wie ächt Religiöse im Herzen" (XIII, 225). Certainly it would have been more pious to leave the statues buried in the earth.

What would seem to be implied here is the pervasive view held by early modern Europe of classical antiquity as a Golden Age, in comparison with which modern men are hypercivilized pygmies. But this is in fact not the case, for the art of the ancients is in fact a distortion of nature. Nature left to herself produces not ideal beauty, but disharmony and distortion; if nature had begun with the perfect little toe of Apollo's statue, it would undoubtedly have gone on to produce a cripple (XIII, 226). Earlier, in the "Creator's" monologue, we are told that the step from nature to the construction of images of the gods represents a diminution of natural piety:

In der einen Sekunde, die sie [die Puppe, d.h., der Mensch] das goldene Zeitalter nannte, schnitzte sie Figuren lieblich anzuschauen und baute Häuserchen darüber, deren Trümmer man in der andern Sekunde anstaunte und als die Wohnung der Götter betrachtete. (IX, 162-163)

But the idea of the "Naturtorso" mentioned in X is in some sense adumbrated in the "Dithyrambus über den Frühling" in this night-watch, where we see how the continuum of nature breaks off abruptly and incomprehensibly at the point where man enters the picture. What, then, is the proper object of harmonious piety? The intellectual constructions of modern man? No. The sculptured images of the Golden Age? No. Nature? No. We see that Bonaventura has shattered the pattern of reality so that man has no truly religious recourse left to him.

That this train of thought should drive the watchman again to the edge of terror is thus not surprising; in the candlelight the statues seem to come to life, but it is only the meaningless movement of a "Torso". Sölle-Nipperdey makes a useful observation on this final scene:

Auf andere Weise wird das Totsein der Götter ins Bewußtsein gerückt. . . . Durch den Hinweis auf die Verstümmelung der Götter schlägt das erhabene Bild ins Groteske um. Hier berühren sich Tod und Leben am nächsten. Der Titan Prometheus bewegt nur noch die Armstümpfe – der Lebensschaffende ist tot – und doch lebendig, aber in grotesker Gebärde. . . . Einen Augenblick lang waren die Götter nah, lebendig, wirkend – aber das Wort fehlt, und zurück bleibt die gespentische Stille.[13]

At the end we see the Furies in threatening immobility; the apparent revivification of the ancient figures turns out to be a pernicious delusion.

For some time now we have been waiting for the "Wonnemonat im Tollhaus" which was promised to us in IX. At the beginning of XIV Bonaventura takes note of our expectation:

Kehre mit mir zurück ins Tollhaus, du stiller Begleiter, der du mich bei meinen Nachtwachen umgiebst. –
Du erinnerst dich noch an meine [sic] Narrenkämmerchen, wenn du anders den Faden meiner Geschichte – die sich still und verborgen, wie ein schmaler Strom, durch die Fels- und Waldstücke, die ich umher aufhäufte, schlingt – nicht verloren hast. (XIV, 230)

In the madhouse the watchman meets an old acquaintance: a girl who played Ophelia to the watchman's Hamlet, and who was so impressed by "die mächtige Hand des Shakespear" (XIV, 232),

---

[13] Sölle-Nipperdey, p. 60.

that her histrionic madness became real, and it became necessary to commit her. Here the watchman, who fears and distrusts love, nevertheless falls in love with her, much against his will. For a time it seems possible to make a compromise with the hollow world in which he is so uneasy. But this final opportunity is torn away from him, for Ophelia gives birth to a dead child and then dies herself. Thus the fourth cycle ends in a tragedy of profound proportions. But it is not Ophelia's tragedy, for in death she recognizes the only possibility of recovering her true identity: "Gottlob daß ich aus dem Stücke herauskomme und meinen angenommenen Namen ablegen kann; hinter dem Stücke geht das Ich an!" (XIV, 252). It is the watchman's tragedy, for out of the depth of his melancholy insights he has made an existential leap, a sort of investment in compromise, and he lands – just where he was before. The flicker of hope which of all things in his life showed the most promise turned out to be also hopeless illusion. Any remaining possibility for the watchman to rejoin the human race and accommodate himself to the human condition has now been permanently eradicated.

It is clear and evident that this chapter is not only the catastrophic culmination of the fourth cycle, according to the pattern we have described, but that it is also the climax of the *Nachtwachen*. Later on we shall see in detail how all the previous thirteen night-watches have been moving in the direction of this one, circuitously, cyclically, but inexorably. In a sense, it is XIV which, under these circumstances, defines the nature of the whole work, for from this point on the watchman's position can no longer be open to doubt; the rest is commentary.

6. Thus it follows that to a certain extent XV and part of XVI are epilogue. The fifteenth night-watch resumes the thread of the watchman's biography, describing his career as a marionetteer. The chapter is replete with satire; we have already had a slap at the chaos of the French Revolution (XII, 210-211), and now the lash is directed against the other political extreme, the official panic which the Revolution caused in Germany. A performance of "Judith and Holofernes" arouses the populace to demand the

head of the local mayor; although the watchman succeeds in quieting the mob, the marionette equipment is confiscated as politically dangerous and the director hangs himself. The narrative brings the biography up to the present, for it is after this event that the narrator becomes a watchman.

But the position of true satire has long since been abandoned, and we see how quickly it fades into the catastrophic gloom which the work has presented with increasing frequency. Not only the unhappy death of the director and the additional failure in the watchman's career, but also the re-introduction of the marionette motif, with which the watchman quiets the mob by denying free will, show that satire and comedy are not and can no longer be the operative force in the work.

The final night-watch contains three anecdotes, all of which, appropriately enough, turn on the question of the meaning of death. The first is a dream of the watchman stimulated by the appearance of a poet whom he meets wandering through the cemetery. The poet attempts to write a poem on immortality, using, ironically enough, a skull as a writing table. As he calls forth a vision of the Day of Judgment, the graves open, but the dead refuse to move. "Wie, ist denn kein Gott!" (XVI, 277) is his horrified cry. The second describes a strange character who claims to be able to see a vision of the dead person above the grave as the body has not decomposed. He has returned for a tryst with his dead beloved. This passage certainly seems influenced by the vision which Novalis calls up in his third "Hymne an die Nacht"; the difference is, however, that Novalis' vision is an intimation of immortality, whereas here the vision gradually fades along with the decomposition of the body into nothingness.

The third anecdote of XVI supplies the final piece to the biographical puzzle. In the cemetery the watchman meets an old gypsy woman, who introduces him to the grave of his father and informs him of the circumstances of his birth. The gypsy opens the grave for him, and there he sees the body of his father un-decomposed. For a moment the watchman believes he can infer a last possibility of permanence in the face of nothingness. But as he attempts to tear apart his father's hands which are folded in a position of prayer, the whole body collapses at once into dust and ashes. It is the final catastrophe, the final victory of death over love, the final evidence for the meaninglessness of being:

Ich streue diese Handvoll väterlichen Staub in die Lüfte und es bleibt
– Nichts!
   Drüben auf dem Grabe steht noch der Geisterseher und umarmt
Nichts!
   Und der Wiederhall im Gebeinhause ruft zum letztenmale –
N i c h t s ! (XVI, 296)

Thus, true to the pattern of the work, this final section ends in a catastrophe which expressly puts the proper label on all the catastrophes preceding, and on the world which has been described here: *Nichts*.

It has been my purpose in this chapter to identify a pattern in the order of the sixteen night-watches. We have found that there is such a pattern, a movement from satire to nihilistic catastrophe, repeated five times over, and we have at least had a suggestion that this pattern is a key to the structure and meaning of the work as a whole. I have tried to stay as close as possible to the relation of the external events to each other, leaving the content and purport to the subsequent discussion, and treating the implications of the events with the greatest brevity, in order to give a clear picture of the whole. It is now necessary to dig a little deeper beneath the surface of the external events and, with the pattern of the work in mind, to attempt an answer to two questions: first, what kind of a personality is the watchman, and how is his development presented to us, and second, how is this personality and his world view presented to us artistically within the structure just described? These questions will occupy our attention in the next two chapters.

III. THE WATCHMAN

How did the watchman arrive at this pass? What is the nature of a man's life and thinking which can carry him to the extreme position presented in the *Nachtwachen*? Are we dealing here with a mind distorted under psychological pressure, or is the nihilism and abysmal pessimism of the watchman drawn existentially from an overall view of life and the world? To answer these questions we shall depart for the time being from a purely structural approach to the work and turn our attention more explicitly to the *Gehalt,* particularly to the biographical background and development of the watchman which is antecedent to the present narration of the novel. If it is true, as has been suggested in the preceding chapter, that the work shows evidence of conscious artistic organization, then it is by no means inappropriate to inquire whether such biographical background as we are given has a coherence and a relevance to the work as a whole. To define the quality of this coherence and the extent of this relevance is the aim of the present chapter.

The story of the watchman's life begins in XVI with the account of the circumstances of his birth given by his mother. For reasons which will become clear later on, however, it will be useful to postpone a discussion of that material for the time being. The beginnings of the watchman's conscious recollection are to be found in IV, where he leafs through a quaint "Lesebuch" of his life, complete with illustrative woodcuts. It is possible that this device is one of the author's innumerable literary jokes, and is meant to be a parody of the similar device in Novalis' *Heinrich von Ofterdingen.* But its effect in this chapter is to produce an ironic distance between the adult watchman and the child he once was; it is as though he were incapable of bridging that gulf without the assistance of a written source (it appears to be largely a product of his foster father), for we are struck in this record of his earliest youth by a freer, brighter, more innocent atmosphere than that of most of the rest of the work. The only other section of the work which invites comparison with this is the account of the blind boy's childhood in XI, where the same kind of childlike innocence and open receptivity to the world around is described. In both cases, we observe, the passages are reproductions of someone else's account; in IV, of the foster father; in XI, of the "Unbekannter im Mantel". The watchman appears himself to have lost the capacity for viewing the world in this manner. His own mordant glosses on the material in the "Lesebuch" illustrate this perfectly:

Gleich auf dem ersten Blatte sieht es bedenklich aus, und pagina V handelt nicht von meiner Geburt, sondern vom Schatzgraben. Hier sieht man mystische Zeichen, aus der Kabbala und auf dem erklärenden Holzschnitte einen nicht gewöhnlichen Schuhmacher, der das Schuhmachen aufgeben will, um Gold machen zu lernen. (IV, 45)

There is a certain amount of mystification in this remark which defies explanation. What exactly is "auf dem ersten Blatte", and on paginae II-IV? Is it a description of the circumstances of the watchman's birth? If so, we are in some difficulty with our assumption that the event in XVI is a revelation which is subsequent to all the other material in the work (see pp. 34-35 above). On the other hand, the word "bedenklich" may merely indicate that he does not himself understand what is described "auf dem ersten Blatte". In any case, however, this is a side issue; what is significant is that the material in XVI is presented last from the perspective of the reader.

Of interest to us is the account of childhood given here and the contrast it presents with the rest of the work. We can begin with the paragraph which describes the third woodcut:

Hier ist ein gewiegter Kommentator von Nöthen. – Auf einem Buche sitze ich, aus einem lese ich; mein Adoptiv-Vater beschäftigt sich mit einem Schuhe, scheint aber zugleich eigenen Betrachtungen über die Unsterblichkeit Raum zu geben. Das Buch worauf ich sitze, enthält Hans Sachsens Fastnachtsspiele, das woraus ich lese, ist Jakob Böhmens Morgenröthe, sie sind der Kern aus unserer Hausbibliothek, weil beide Verfasser zunftfähige Schuhmacher und Poeten waren. (IV, 47)

If we attempt ourselves to be the required "gewiegter Kommentator", we notice at once several interesting things. First of all, we cannot explain the oddities of the watchman on the basis of his upbringing or from the personality of his foster father. Despite his hobby of alchemy and his propensity for brooding over deep matters, and even though he remains where "ein anderer ehrlicher Mann von Handwerke liefe bei solchen Umgebungen davon" (IV, 46), the old shoemaker is by no means an ominous figure. Both his own words and his actions in caring for the foundling show him to be one of the few examples of ordinary human kindness in the *Nachtwachen*. Nowhere is there an indication that his impact on the boy was in the least oppressive. From this fact an important conclusion can be drawn which may be usefully kept in mind throughout the remainder of this discussion: the *Nachtwachen* is not a psychological novel. However we may account for the peculiar state of the watchman's mind, it is not explained in the novel as the result of psychological conditioning. This observation is not irrelevant for two reasons. First, we have just exactly such a psychological novel in the previous decade; it is Karl Philipp Moritz's *Anton Reiser* (1790-95), about which more will be said in Chapter V. Secondly, the lack of psychological determination indicates that basically the watchman's position is not to be regarded as an aberration, as a unique and pitiable incapacity to find meaning in the world. We are thus encouraged to take the watchman's position more seriously than we otherwise might.

Returning to our passage, we observe the explicit references to Hans Sachs and Jakob Böhme. This may appear at first sight as a superficial display of literary free association: the shoemaker-poet combination is connected with Sachs and Böhme on the one hand, with the old shoemaker and eventually with Kreuzgang[1] himself on the other. But if we dispose of the passage in this way we once again find ourselves accusing the author of intolerable artistic blundering, for what have the solid bourgeois wit and wisdom of Hans Sachs or the mystical flight, joyful communion with God and symbolic dualism of Böhme to do with the corrosive nihilism of the watchman? Clearly nothing whatever. Let us then entertain the possibility that this is precisely the point, that, taken together, Sachs and Böhme represent the world of clearly defined values and deep religious receptivity which has been left behind by the watchman. Sachs and Böhme then indicate not lasting influences upon Kreuzgang, but aspects of the childhood paradise which is irretrievably lost.

Of this paradise of childhood we hear more immediately. The description which the shoemaker gives of the character of his foundling (IV, 48-52) presents a child totally receptive to the world of nature, a child who can regard the sunrise with imperishable wonder and who comprehends the language of the stars and flowers. At this point we find ourselves most unambiguously in the world of German Romanticism:

Ebenfalls nennt er die Blumen oft eine Schrift, die wir nur nicht zu lesen verständen, desgleichen auch die bunten Gesteine. Er hoft diese Sprache noch einst zu lernen, und verspricht dann gar wundersame Dinge daraus mitzutheilen. Oft behorcht er ganz heimlich die Mükken oder Fliegen wenn sie im Sonnenschein summen, weil er glaubt sie unterredeten sich über wichtige Gegenstände, von denen bis jezt noch kein Mensch etwas ahnete: Schwazt er den Gesellen und Lehrburschen in der Werkstatt dergleichen vor und sie lachen über ihn, so erklärt er sie sehr ernsthaft für Blinde und Taube, die weder sähen noch hörten, was um sie her vorginge. (IV, 49-50)

We need only compare this passage with the opening sentences of one of the archetypal creations of Romanticism, Novalis'

---

[1] The odd name was given to the boy "dem Gebrauche gemäß" (IV, 48), because he was found at a crossroads. Although the contemporary German word for a crossroads was "Kreuzweg", Bonaventura selects the old form because it also has the meaning of a journey beset with tribulation, presumably by analogy to Christ's way to Calvary. See Jakob and Wilhelm Grimm, *Deutches Wörterbuch*, V (Leipzig, 1873), cols. 2191-2.

Lehrlinge zu Sais (1798), in order to identify the ground upon which Bonaventura here stands:

Mannigfache Wege gehen die Menschen. Wer sie verfolgt und vergleicht, wird wunderliche Figuren entstehen sehn; Figuren, die zu jener großen Chiffernschrift zu gehören scheinen, die man überall, auf Flügeln, Eierschalen, in Wolken, im Schnee, in Kristallen und in Steinbildungen, auf gefrierenden Wassern, im Innern und Äußern der Gebirge, der Pflanzen, der Tiere, der Menschen, in den Lichtern des Himmels, auf berührten und gestrichenen Scheiben von Pech und Glas, in den Feilspänen um den Magnet her, und sonderbaren Konjunkturen des Zufalls erblickt. In ihnen ahndet man den Schlüssel dieser Wunderschrift, die Sprachlehre derselben, allein die Ahndung will sich selbst in keine feste Formen fügen und scheint kein höherer Schlüssel werden zu wollen.[2]

This, too, is part of the lost realm. That the adult watchman can still imitate, after a fashion, the language of Novalis, is illustrated by the "Dithyrambus über den Frühling" at the beginning of XIII (pp. 218-220). But this "hymnisch anredende Beschreibung des Frühlings"[3] is now overshadowed and negated by the watchman's pessimistic, nihilistic view of the position of man in the universe. For the adult watchman the hopes which Romanticism placed in direct, inner contact with nature are no longer operative; they belong to the lost paradise of childhood.

Although the abandonment of the natural piety of childhood is not explained within the context of the *Nachtwachen*, the situation is significant from the point of view of Romanticism in general. For in a sense one might say that it is the inability to sustain

---

[2] Novalis, *Schriften*, ed. J. Minor (Jena, 1907), IV, 3. A very clear exposition of the importance which the Romantics assigned to the possibility of understanding the language of nature, particularly in terms of Schelling's nature philosophy, appears in Wolfgang Liepe, "Hebbel und Schelling", *Deutsche Beiträge*, ed. Arnold Bergsträsser (Chicago and Munich, 1953), pp. 121-181, esp. pp. 145-149. A discussion of the development of the notion of hieroglyphics or "Chiffernschrift", which were understood to contain mysteries and wisdom inexpressible in the normal patterns of language, and which the Romantics applied to the phenomena of nature, appears in Lieselotte Dieckmann, "The Metaphor of Hieroglyphics in German Romanticism", *Comparative Literature*, VII (1955), 306-312.

[3] Sölle-Nipperdey, p. 73. She derives Bonaventura's method of dynamic nature description from Jean Paul (*ibid.*, p. 39).

the confident and mystical quality of Novalis' contact with nature which characterizes much of the subsequent development of Romanticism. I have already hinted at this when discussing the dissertation of Sigrid Gölz (see above pp. 28-29). Novalis was able to maintain the integrity of his being along with his infinite yearnings because he was able to maintain, especially in his profession, a meaningful contact with finite, material reality; he had, as it were, a sense for the flesh of nature as well as for its spirit. As the spirit of Romanticism becomes increasingly disembodied, however, the loss of contact with finite reality and, concomitantly, with the integrity of the self, gradually becomes a shattering and terrifying experience, leaving only an unfulfilled and unfulfillable longing for totality and infinitude. Thus, from the point of view of the history of ideas, the crisis displayed in the *Nachtwachen* of 1804 represents an anticipation of the dangers which were to threaten the Romantic mode of thinking.

Though we have come to see that the description of childhood in IV stands in contrast to, rather than in explanation of, the position of the adult watchman, we would be glad to find in this chapter some plausible hint to account for his subsequent development. There is one such hint, which we will be able to follow to some extent throughout the biography: it is Kreuzgang's extraordinarily incisive intelligence. A first suggestion of this is the ironic humility with which he declines to continue his explication of the third woodcut, "weil in dem Holzschnitte von meiner eigenen Originalität zuviel die Rede ist" (IV, 48). But it is graphically brought out in the old shoemaker's description of the boy's method of questioning. The boy begins by asking about the materials of which a shoe is made, and then presses continually on,

... indem er ... über jede einzelne Substanz Aufklärung verlangte, immer höher und höher sich verstieg, erst in die Naturwissenschaften, indem er das Leder auf den Ochsen zurück führte, dann gar noch weiter bis ich mich zulezt mit meinem Schuhe hoch oben in der Theologie befand und er mir grad heraus sagte daß ich in meinem Fache ein Stümper sei, weil ich ihm darin nicht bis zum lezten Grunde Auskunft geben könnte. (IV, 49)

It must be said that this display is related by the foster father with great good humor, and in and of itself might be expected of any bright child. But for the reader familiar with the whole work, this embryonic pressure toward final explanations takes on quite an ominous coloring, because if the end of the striving after basic answers is emptiness (contrast here *Faust*!), and the desire for such answers is so elemental as to be so fully developed in the child as it is for Kreuzgang, then the profundity of the watchman's pessimism becomes more comprehensible.

The thread of biography is resumed again in VII, where a gap of several years is to be understood, since at this point we are no longer dealing with a child, but with a more or less accomplished youth. Kreuzgang has now himself entered the shoemaker-poet pattern and he occupies himself successfully with the composition of occasional verses. But the gap between the two sections is more than a matter of years, because the innocence of childhood has now disappeared without a trace. This is clearly evident in the first of these poetic productions, the "Leichenrede" upon the birth of a child (VII, 114-116). In this facetious monologue, birth is seen as the beginning of a process of dying, and by implication the whole of human life is reduced to a meaningless interlude between birth and death. The impression of life and health made by the infant is a delusion:

Traut auch, ich bitte euch, dem Lebensscheine und den Rosen auf den Wangen des Knaben nicht; das ist die Kunst der Natur, wodurch sie, gleich einem geschikten Arzte, den einbalsamirten Körper eine längere Zeit in einer angenehmen Täuschung erhält; in seinem Innern nagt doch die Verwesung schon. (VII, 114-115)

Thus in Kreuzgang's very first original production we find already the pervasive motif of the *Nachtwachen*: the mask. The life of man is not what it seems to be; later we read, "das Leben ist nur das Schellenkleid das das Nichts umgehängt hat" (VIII, 150); it is a mask covering a core of chaos and meaninglessness, and throughout the work it appears as the task of the watchman to demask life and the world, to lay bare the existential horror beneath. The urge to reveal this insight is fully present at this earliest stage of his career.

How has this happened? What is the bridge that has carried

Kreuzgang from Hans Sachs and Jakob Böhme, from his confident delight in his receptivity to nature, from what is clearly a
by no means unhappy childhood, to this gloomy point? The
answer is that we simply do not know. The stages of development
in the boy's thinking are not presented to us, und thus we see that
we not only do not have a psychological novel; strictly speaking
we do not have a biographical novel at all, at least not an *Ent-
wicklungsroman* after the pattern of Goethe's *Wilhelm Meister,*
because we are given essentially finished conclusions, not their
genesis. In IV Kreuzgang is the Romantic youth par excellence;
in VII he describes himself explicitly as an example of the Titan-
figure of *Sturm und Drang,* a giant who must be restrained under
the weight of a mountain of restricting circumstances. The genesis
of the Titan out of the Romantic youth remains for us a mystery.
This disinclination to present psychological determinants, incidentally, can be regarded as an artistic failure only if we regard the
watchman's final position as an aberration; if however we are
willing to accept as a premise that his views have logical validity
and are the result of the application of an exceptionally alert
intelligence to the world about, we need not miss the lack of
psychological development, for that is not within the purview of
the work.

Though we are not able to say how the position came to be,
we can identify a certain ambivalence and a certain development
within the position itself. The ambivalence appears here for the
first time in the grotesque speculation upon the watchman's origin:

... daß eben der Teufel selbst, um dem Himmel einen Possen zu
spielen, sich während einer dunklen Nacht in das Bette einer kanonisirten Heiligen geschlichen, und da mich gleichsam als eine lex
cruciata[4] für unsern Herrgott niedergeschrieben habe, bei der er sich
am Weltgerichtstage den Kopf zerbrechen solle. (VII, 112)

Here there is at least a hint of dual personality at war with itself,
extreme versions of saintliness and evil in a struggle to form a

---

[4] Further punning on the name Kreuzgang. "Lex cruciata" was a technical term for the law of biological inheritance, according to Andreas
Müller, *Nachtwachen von Bonaventura* (= *Deutsche Literatur in Entwicklungsreihen, Reihe Romantik,* XVI) (Leipzig, 1930), 251.

self. There is a suggestion that at this stage of his life some sort of salvation might still have been possible. The likelihood of further development in the other direction appears in Kreuzgang's immediately subsequent career; he is imprisoned because one of his satires has been taken personally by a worthy citizen. It is to be observed that it is Kreuzgang's fate to be misunderstood; the "Leichenrede" is blithely accepted at face value by the citizenry and used as such under the assumption that Kreuzgang had simply been mistaken in referring it to the birth of an infant. Thus at the very beginning of the watchman's career we see his fatal divergence from normal human patterns of thinking: "Eins ist nur möglich; entweder stehen die Menschen verkehrt, oder ich. Wenn die Stimmenmehrheit hier entscheiden soll; so bin ich rein verloren" (VII, 113), not to mention the misunderstanding the child Kreuzgang experiences from his fellows when he claims to hear the language of nature (cf. p. 61 above). And indeed, the second misunderstanding, that of the satire, does have serious consequences. He is confined in the tower,

wo ich Muße hatte immer wilder zu werden. Dabei gings mir übrigens mit meinem Menschenhasse wie den Fürsten, die den einzelnen Menschen wohlthun, und sie nur in ganzen Heeren würgen. (VII, 120)

Thus while we are not privy to the original genesis of the watchman's views, we are able to see them develop and deepen. It is worth noting that this is the first time the word "Menschenhaß" appears in the work; nevertheless, we see that a certain ambivalence is still present, because the possibility of "den einzelnen Menschen wohlthun" still exists.

Upon his release from prison Kreuzgang becomes a *Bänkelsänger* and quickly turns from "Schlachtstücken" and "Mordgeschichten" to aggressive contemporary satire, wherein the watchman stresses the violence of his own attitudes:

... ich fing an mich zu den nüzlichen Mitgliedern im Staate, als zu den Fechtmeistern, Gewehrfabrikanten, Pulvermüllern, Kriegsministern, Aerzten u.s.w., die alle offenbar dem Tode in die Hand arbeiten, zu zählen, und bekam eine gute Meinung von mir, indem ich meine Zuhörer und Schüler abzuhärten, und sie an blutige Auftritte zu gewöhnen mich bemühete. (VII, 122)

This satirical violence does not recede even when he is hauled before a court charged with slander. Here he twits the judges behind their "Gerechtigkeitsmasken" by suggesting that in order properly to understand crime and apprehend criminals they ought themselves to engage in crime, with the implication, of course, that they in fact do so. The result for Kreuzgang is incarceration in the madhouse. Gradually a pattern of destructiveness has unfolded which makes Kreuzgang totally oblivious of his own self-interest. He has become a sort of prophet in reverse, urging upon the world at whatever cost to himself his insights into the chaotic and meaningless ground of the universe.

The madhouse itself is the subject of the ninth night-watch. The symbol of the madhouse is of considerable complexity and, like so many other things in the *Nachtwachen,* it is all but impossible to assign a consistent value to it. That it is a concentrated reflection of the world at large is made clear at the beginning of IX:

Eben so ist es mit dem allgemeinen Irrhause, aus dessen Fenstern so viele Köpfe schauen, theils mit partiellem, theils mit totalem Wahnsinne; auch in dieses sind noch kleinere Tollhäuser für besondere Narren hineingebaut. In eins von diesen kleinern brachten sie mich jezt aus dem großen, vermuthlich weil sie dieses für zu stark besezt hielten. Ich fand es indeß hier gerade wie dort; ja fast noch besser, weil die fixe Idee der mit mir eingesperrten Narren meistens eine angenehme war. (IX, 154-155)

All the same, it is not possible to regard the madhouse as a vehicle of affirmation in contrast to a denial of the world without. Here we are in a situation which reminds us of the watchman's remark that he frequently found himself laughing in churches and praying in brothels. This is not to say that the brothel particularly represents a value which is missing in the church; it is simply a reflection of the watchman's total perversion of thinking, in which concepts and values contrast and clash wildly with one another without being able to come to rest in any stable, comprehensible order, which is in turn a reflection of the existential perversity of the world. Similarly, in the madhouse we find not only more or less positive figures who have come to grief in their conflict with the senselessness of the world (e.g., the various poets, the orator, the lovers, the victim of an official theft), but also figures who are themselves the object of the watchman's shrill satire (e.g., the idealist and realist philosophers, the courtier who imagines himself a dog and the official who has become a wolf). Thus, though it is true that "das Gemeinsame zwischen sehr vielen von ihnen und dem Nachtwächter ist, daß ihnen das Tagleben transparent wird",[5] nonetheless the madhouse is by and large a miniature of the world without, and we search in vain for an indication of positive value in it.

This observation presents us with a certain amount of difficulty when we turn to the God of this miniature world, the ninth inmate. The burden of his monologue is the incongruity of the human being with the rest of Creation (cf. XIII, 219). By giving man a spark of divine reason, God has confused the clear, well-organized distinction between creator and creature. On the basis of this speck of reason, man has arrogated to himself the role of a critic of God and Creation, and has put himself into such disharmony with the nature that God repents himself of this aspect of his creation without being able to decide just what is to be done about it. Some of this reminds us rather forcibly of Mephisto's lines in the "Prolog im Himmel":

> Der kleine Gott der Welt bleibt stets von gleichem Schlag,
> Und ist so wunderlich als wie am ersten Tag.
> Ein wenig besser würd' er leben,
> Hättst du ihm nicht den Schein des Himmelslichts gegeben;
> Er nennt's Vernunft und braucht's allein,
> Nur tierischer als jedes Tier zu sein (*Faust* I, ll. 281-286),

lines which were presumably reposing in Goethe's desk at the time when the *Nachtwachen* was written. But the presentation in the *Nachtwachen* presupposes in turn a God whose creative hand is unsure: "als ich es [das Sonnenstäubchen, d.h., den Menschen] geschaffen hatte, sagte ich zwar der Sonderbarkeit wegen es sei gut – übereilt war das freilich, indeß ich hatte nun einmal meine gute Laune" (IX, 161). In order to attempt some evaluation of this passage, we can regard it in three steps:

　　1) The "Creator" is a madman, an inmate in a madhouse. Like

---

[5] Sölle-Nipperdey, p. 65.

many of the other inmates, he has lost his senses in a clash with
the senselessness of the world, and now his delusion that he is
God permits him to release his misanthropic gall over mankind
in general. Seen from this standpoint, his views are not normative,
but the result of mental aberration; what is here pointed up is the
state of the world which has brought him to this pass. Kreuzgang
himself comments upon the "Creator's" monologue, with typical
ambiguity, "Was das für ein verruchter Wahnsinn ist. . . . Wenn
ein vernünftiger Mensch dergleichen vorbrächte, würde man es
wahrlich konfisziren" (IX, 164).

2) We recall, however, that some of the inmates are more or
less positive figures. Nowhere is the "Creator" an object of satire
as are certain other inmates. It is therefore possible that the
attitudes and insights of the "Creator" are substantially correct;
that this is the result of a panoramic view of Creation from a
cosmic standpoint.

3) If this is so, and if we remember that the madhouse is
meant to be a miniature of the world, then it is likely that the
"Creator" is in fact a God-figure, essentially the same kind of
God who appears as the "Marionettendirekteur" in IV. We thus
reach a point from which much of the *Gehalt* of the *Nachtwachen*
can be satisfactorily explained: a profound loss of faith in God.
This is not the same as a loss of *belief* in God, for which there
are perhaps remedies; God still exists in the world as drawn by
Bonaventura, but he is no longer to be loved, no longer to be
trusted, no longer even to be feared, for if Creation displays his
handiwork, one can only conclude from it that God is a pathetic
bungler, like a decrepit old man. The "Creator's" indecision,
his petulance, even his "Hörrohr" illustrate this view. This is
apparently the view attained by the young Kreuzgang, and a conviction more devoid of the possibility of consolation or more
replete with existential terror would be hard to imagine. If this
interpretation appears chaotic and somewhat self-contradictory,
it is not primarily because the work itself is chaotic and somewhat
self-contradictory (although it is), but because the world as
represented in the work has these qualities. One of the chief
characteristics of the work and its world is the lack of conceptual

stability, a matter about which we shall have more to say in the next chapter.

Against such a background the wisdom of man can lead only to absurdity and eventually to death. Kreuzgang passes his time in his cell by drawing parallels between Socrates and Scaramouche, the buffoon from the *Commedia dell' Arte,* in which the buffoon comes out best, for the absurdities of a fool reflect the world more accurately than even the skepticism of Socrates. This persistent adulation of the fool in Romanticism generally and in the *Nachtwachen* in particular has been noted by Werner Kohlschmidt:

Seine Existenz ist, anders als bei Grimmelshausen, sozusagen Anti-Existenz. Sie bildet sich aus den Gegensätzen zum Bürgerlichen, zum Kleinlichen, Begrenzten, Normalen, Ordentlichen. Ihre Position kann höchstens in der Freiheit des phantastischen Daseins liegen, das aber zugleich Unverbindlichkeit nach allen Seiten hin ist.[6]

So much for absurdity; as for death, Kreuzgang relates to the doctor in charge of the madhouse that he at one time conceived the plan of earning three doctorates, so that as a physician he might kill his patient, as a lawyer order his affairs, and as a theologian show him the path to the next world; all three faculties are merely in the service of death in the long run. This can lead only to an inextricable confusion of categories:

Ja, wer entscheidet es zuletzt, ob wir Narren hier in dem Irrhause meisterhafter irren, oder die Fakultisten in den Hörsälen? Ob vielleicht nicht gar Irrthum, Wahrheit; Narrheit, Weisheit; Tod, Leben ist – wie man vernünftigerweise es dermalen gerade im Gegentheile nimmt! – O ich bin inkurabel, das sehe ich selbst ein. (IX, 172-173)

It is interesting to observe the doctor's response to all this: he prescribes "wenig oder gar kein Denken", because Kreuzgang's condition is caused by "übertriebene intellektuelle Schwelgerei" (IX, 173). The only possibility of a cure, it would seem, is to anesthetize that penetrating intellect which from Kreuzgang's earliest youth has sliced through the veil of illusion surrounding the world.

[6] "Nihilismus der Romantik", *Form und Innerlichkeit* (Bern, 1955), p. 173.

The ambivalence mentioned earlier finds its resolution in the next section of biographical material, the love affair in XIV. We recall the indications that there remains yet a saintly element in Kreuzgang, and still a possibility for individual human relationship. These possibilities are now to be explored and eradicated. Kreuzgang's original reaction to the madness of the actress is chilling in its detachment:

Für mich war es ein *interessantes* Schauspiel, dieses gewaltige Eingreifen einer Riesenhand in ein fremdes Leben, dieses Umschaffen der wirklichen Person zu einer poetischen, die jetzt vor den Augen aller Vernünftigen, auf Kothurnen ernsthaft auf- und abging, und abgerissene Gesänge, wie wunderbare Geistersprüche, hören ließ. (XIV, 232) (Italics mine.)

This icy insensitivity, however, yields rapidly to a feeling of true love when he finds her as his neighbor in the madhouse. The meaning of love in this context is made clear by the description of its first symptom: Kreuzgang conceives a plan to establish a colony of fools and madmen, "zum Schrecken der andern vernünftigen Menschen" (XIV, 233). In other words, the first effect of love is a breakdown in Kreuzgang's total isolation from mankind, the isolation which only a short time before permitted him to speak of deep suffering as an "interessantes Schauspiel". It is true that he is still talking of fools and of opposing the reasonable world, but the important thing is that the first attack of love releases in him what is apparently a slumbering desire for contact, to reach out beyond himself and to invest in a relationship with human beings.

Kreuzgang's intellectual response to this possibility is fear. He sees in love the danger of falling victim to just that kind of delusion which has been held up to ridicule all this time. It is not only a fear of compromising his principles; it is a fear of being himself deluded into making a leap into that chaos of meaninglessness which he has already identified. All this is expressed in his composition "An die Liebe" ("in der That, ich halte dein wahres Gesicht nicht für das reizendste", XIV, 237), in his equation of hatred with freedom, and health and love with slavery and sickness (XIV, 241), in his identification of love as the invention of the Devil to conceal the true nature of the world (XIV, 242). Despite all this, he is driven, in his strange, negative fashion, to court the love of Ophelia. Apparently there is in him, alongside of his capacity for intellectual perception, a powerful desire to deny all he knows, perhaps even permanently, by means of a love-relationship. He is able for a time to *stop thinking,* as the doctor has recommended: ". . . ich konnte in gewissen Stunden aus einem Loche meiner Kaukasushöle schauen, und weniger denken als nichts" (XIV, 234). The result of not thinking is a weakening of the effect of his tormenting ideas:

. . . ich fing gar an in mich vertieft umherzuwandern, und fühlte mich fast human und kleinlaut gegen die Welt gestimmt. Einmal meinte ich gar, sie könnte doch wohl die beste sein, und der Mensch selbst wäre etwas mehr, als das erste Thier darauf, ja er habe einigen Werth und könne vielleicht gar unsterblich sein. (XIV, 238-239)

Ophelia's problem is somewhat different; she has lost her identity. She is unable to pin down an enduring reality: "Giebt es etwas an sich, oder ist alles nur Wort und Hauch und viel Phantasie?" (XIV, 243). In the midst of this chaotic, undefinable reality she is unable to comprehend the terms of her own existence; and she too has recognized the essentially masked character of the world:

Sieh da kann ich mich nimmer herausfinden, ob ich ein Traum – ob es nur Spiel, oder Wahrheit, und ob die Wahrheit wieder mehr als Spiel – eine Hülse sitzt über der andern, und ich bin oft auf dem Punkte den Verstand darüber zu verlieren. (XIV, 243-244)

Now Kreuzgang-Hamlet finds himself in the unaccustomed role of a purveyor of consolation, and this puts him in an awkward position. While still maintaining his conviction that the self ends in nothingness, and rejecting all ontological speculation as mean-ingless ("Ich hätte das Sein erst um das Sein selbst befragen sollen, dann ließe sich nachher auch über das Nichtsein etwas Gescheutes ausmitteln", XIV, 247), he must yet urge Ophelia to play the game. Kreuzgang's fanatical adherence to the bitter truth seems to have eased somewhat, for though he recommends that they have a child "blos aus Rache, damit nach uns noch Rollen auftreten müssen, die alle diese Langweiligkeiten von neuem [sic] ausweiten" (*ibid.*), this is hardly to be credited; he is now fighting hard to maintain his convictions in the face of the emotion which has engulfed him.

The death of Ophelia and their child bring different solutions to the two problems. Death seems to have restored to Ophelia her lost self; on the threshold of death she regains the shattered integrity of her personality and is now able to say with conviction, as she could not say before, that she truly loves Kreuzgang. For Kreuzgang it is the tragic end of ambivalence; the competing possibility that there might be value, meaning, communion in life is now destroyed. He, too, has had a vision which has brought him face to face with his self in the night of Ophelia's death, but it is a vision of total terror and nihilism:

Kein Gegenstand war ringsum aufzufinden, als das große schreckliche Ich, das an sich selbst zehrte, und im Verschlingen stets sich wiedergebar. ... Die Abwechselung war zugleich mit der Zeit verschwunden, und es herrschte eine fürchterliche ewig öde Langeweile. (XIV, 251)

The hesitating experiment with meaning, pessimistically undertaken, has ended in abysmal failure, leaving only an unrelieved deepening of his previous position, now approaching the most negative kind of solipsism.[7] The extent of his emotional investment in this matter is illustrated by the fact that the demonic laughter which is his usual response to the world is stifled at this point and replaced by the first tear of his life.

Sölle-Nipperdey makes an interesting stylistic observation on this chapter to illustrate the seriousness of the event. At the beginning of the love affair the watchman can still afford to indulge in that ironic play of words which reminds one of Heine: "Hinter diesem Briefwechsel trat nun unser Wortwechsel ein, und jeder

---

[7] On the subject of this isolation of the ego, cf. Joachim Müller, "Die Nachtwachen von Bonaventura", *Neue Jahrbücher für Wissenschaft und Jugendbildung,* XII (1936), 442: "Wer sich vollends auf sich selbst zurückziehen will, sein Ich sucht, sein Ich anschauen will, findet nur schreckliche Einsamkeit im Ich. Auch das Ich ist dann nur Illusion, ist nicht mehr Besinnung auf die Notwendigkeit des Existenzansatzes; denn es stellt die Fragwürdigkeit des Alleinseins vor den Anspruch der Welt, der nur im Gebundensein der Schicksalsgemeinschaft beantwortet werden kann."

nachfolgende Wechsel, von den Blicken, Küssen und dergleichen an, bis zum Selbstwechsel" (XIV, 249). Of this Sölle-Nipperdey says:

> Zu Beginn dieser Liebe ist solch ironischer Bericht noch möglich. . . . Je näher aber das tragische Ende der Geschichte rückt . . ., desto reflexionsloser wird einfach berichtet. Hier wird die Welt als geschehende Wirklichkeit so unmittelbar erfahren, daß keine Reflexion mehr nötig ist, um das Nichts hinter ihr zu enthüllen. Der Bericht genügt sich. Die Verdichtung, die dadurch erreicht wird, ist für die *Nachtwachen* selten und ergreifend.[8]

In passing it ought to be said that XIV is a most eloquent example of the impact of Shakespeare upon the Germany of this period. It has been said that "Shakespeare's 'problem' . . . is that of imparting order and poetic significance to the keenly felt but separate elements of human experience".[9] The German imagination, however, seems to have been caught less by Shakespeare's resolutions of the problem than by his statement of the problem itself. For the type of German mind represented by Bonaventura, Hamlet's famous question "To be or not to be" is not the reaction of a particular man to a particular situation, the despairing response of a man caught in a ferocious dilemma of conflicting loyalties and lacking the resources of will to deal with it; it is the pertinent question posed by the human condition in general. For the watchman the choice between being and not being is dependent upon the extent to which one can comprehend and place a value upon being: "Ich hätte das Sein erst um das Sein selbst befragen sollen, dann ließe sich nachher auch über das Nichtsein etwas Gescheutes ausmitteln" (XIV, 247). If however the disparate elements of reality cannot somehow be bridged, then Hamlet's question, posed in this way, defies solution and becomes permanent, thus blocking any path to the meaning of life. The specific "modernity" (if one may use the term) of the Romantics and of Bonaventura especially consists partly in their recognition of modern man's fragmented apprehension of being, and thus it is small wonder

---

[8] Sölle-Nipperdey, p. 32.

[9] D. A. Traversi, *An Approach to Shakespeare*, 2d edn. (Garden City, New York, 1956), p. 286.

that they found themselves fascinated by Shakespeare's "keenly felt but separate elements of human experience". Whether or not this is a correct interpretation of Shakespeare is of course beside the point. The extent of the watchman's identification with the problem as conceived in this way is evident in XIV in a progressively unfolding pattern. His motive for playing Hamlet in the first place was "Ingrimm über die Menschheit . . ., um Gelegenheit zu haben, mich gegen das schweigend dasitzende Parterre eines Theils meiner Galle zu entledigen" (XIV, 231); thus in a curious twist on Aristotle the performance of a tragedy becomes a catharsis for the actor rather than the audience. But the girl produces a more total response; her "real" personality disintegrates under the pressure of Shakespeare's problem. The extent of the watchman's identification with the situation is shown by the fact that he continues to style himself "Hamlet" during the love affair. This is much more than a matter of simply playing the game and humoring Ophelia; he has dissociated Hamlet's despair from its particular context and found in it a deep affinity to his own situation. All this illustrates the extremely labile nature of the condition in which the watchman finds himself in his love affair, and explains the depth of the catastrophe when the experiment fails.[10]

In night-watch XV we see the end product of these events. "Ich hatte aus dem Tollhause einen verstärkten Haß gegen alle Vernünftige mitgebracht, die mit ihren platten nichtssagenden Physiognomien, jezt wieder um und neben mir wandelten" (XV, 256), and "Ich war recht froh and frei und haßte die Menschen nach Belieben, weil sie so klein und nichtsnutzig durch den grossen Sonnentempel hinschlichen" (XV, 257). Here we get also an explanation of the watchman's satirical position; laughter is the only possible response to the absurdity of life and the world. It is significant

---

[10] Werner Kohlschmidt's study, "Das Hamlet-Motiv in den 'Nachtwachen' des Bonaventura", *German Studies Presented to Walter Horace Bruford* (London, 1962), pp. 163-175, appeared after my own interpretation was written. Rather than attempt to introduce Kohlschmidt's insights into my discussion, I refer the reader to his whole essay, which is one of the most penetrating and enlightening examinations of the *Nachtwachen* ever written.

that the moon, to which Kreuzgang under the influence of love dedi-
cated a good-humored monologue (XIV, 234-236), is now singled
out explicitly as worthy of satirical laughter (XV, 260). Laughter,
like love, is an invention of the Devil. But though the Devil invented love to vex and delude man, he has provided laughter,
under deceptive auspices, to be sure, to unmask the world. Here
it would seem that God is the deceiver and the Devil the apostle
of truth. This passage demonstrates fully that the ubiquitous
satires of the *Nachtwachen* are not present merely for their own
sake, to hold up certain aspects of the world to ridicule; they are
a thoroughgoing and indeed inescapable response to the basic
delusion of life. "Dieses Lachen erst ist der Triumph des Sub-
jektivismus. Aber es ist zugleich das Lachen einer letzten, schauer-
lichen Einsamkeit." [11]

In this chapter Kreuzgang makes one final attempt to pursue
his poetic vocation. That the possibility of inner salvation is gone
beyond recall is shown by the speech with which he prevents the
revolutionary populace from beheading the mayor. No appeal to
morality or to the virtues of bourgeois order is made. He simply
points out that the mayor, like the marionette Holofernes and
every other creature, is not to be held responsible for his acts,
because there is no freedom of will; all action is simply a meaningless movement in a chaos of unseen forces. The collapse of Kreuzgang's final vocational endeavor represents, as it were, his final
and total separation from the human race, and the decision to
become night watchman represents a profound personal bitterness.
It is pathetic in the extreme that Kreuzgang weeps his second tear
over the confiscated Hanswurst; his truncated capacity for love
has been transferred to a lifeless marionette, to a wooden vehicle
for nonsense and satire. Yet even that is taken from him.

We have postponed until this point the account of the watchman's birth given in the final night-watch. The reason for this is
that the account is clearly not on the same level of realism as the

---

[11] H. A. Korff, *Geist der Goethezeit,* 2d edn. (Leipzig, 1949), III, 228.
The sentence continues: "... die in einem wirklichen Menschen gedacht
und nicht in einer bloßen Marionette – nichts anderes als der Wahnsinn
ist." Here I am not at all in agreement.

remainder of the biographical narration. To be sure, "realism", insofar as it can be applied at all to the *Nachtwachen,* can only be used relatively. The degree of psychological and material plausibility of the events throughout the *Nachtwachen* is rather low. But they do not partake of the supernatural. The frequent references to the Devil, for instance, are allegorical glosses upon the action and not events in themselves. Therefore the sixteenth night-watch is probably to be understood also as a more or less allegorical or symbolic explanation of the work despite the fact that its action merges into the more realistic level of the work at the point where the shoemaker finds the casket with the infant in it. The scene in the cemetery, however, makes no attempt whatever at realistic plausibility; besides the supernatural elements surrounding Kreuzgang's birth, there is no explanation as to how his long-lost mother recognized him in the cemetery, and both parties evince very little surprise at the moment of reunion.

What does it mean that the watchman's father was a godless black magician, his mother a gypsy, and that the Devil stood godfather at the moment of conception? The watchman himself calls it "ein gefährlicher psychologischer Schlüssel" (XIV, 281). We must try not to misunderstand this remark; we have insisted elsewhere that the watchman's personality, as presented in the novel, is not psychologically determined in the modern sense of the word. Indeed, the watchman himself expresses doubt about the capacity of psychologists to anatomize "einen so hypothetischen Gegenstand, als die Seele ist" (XVI, 281-282), in the very next paragraph. We must take the word "psychologisch" in a more general sense as referring to the state of the watchman's soul; "ein psychologischer Schlüssel" means that the circumstances of his birth are an explanation of his condition, but we must understand it as an allegorical, not a cause-and-effect explanation. It is *as though* the hour of conception were marked by the exorcism of demons, *as though* the Devil had stood godfather to him, *as though* he displayed an external similarity to the Devil (XVI, 280). It is as though a curse were placed upon him, a congenital affinity to the powers of darkness which accounts for the inexplicable transformation from the childhood paradise of

IV to the frightful insights of VII. We shall have occasion to return to this final night-watch in the next chapter; here we need only call attention to the way in which this passage underlines the inescapable and unrelievedly black quality of the watchman's insights; the myth of the "eben kanonisirte Heilige" is totally discredited; the possibility of ambivalence, that is to say, of hope, is gone, and we are left only with the stark and unadulterated nihilism of the watchman.

In summary, it is important to be clear about the attitude of the watchman who begins to narrate the night-watches. We have seen it develop through intellectual perception and the disappointment of other possibilities to essentially the following view: life, or man's life in the world, at any rate, is a delusion, a series of masks thrown over a core of chaotic meaninglessness. Life is not only transitory, ending in death; it is so meaningless that an afterlife would be a prospect horrible beyond description. The loving, all-wise, trustworthy God of the Judeo-Christian tradition is gone; in his place is a fumbler who has spoiled his Creation, which harbors also the Devil, with his malicious laughter. In the midst of this howling chaos cowers the ego, consuming itself to no purpose, and able only to retain its integrity by calling attention constantly to the true condition of reality. This position of the watchman's is stable, complete and unrelieved at the beginning of the first night-watch. Thus the cyclical pattern which we have identified in the preceding chapter is purely an artificial superstructure imposed upon the material. It is artistic structuring of the most elementary kind, aimed directly at the reader, and is in no way congruent with the structure of the genesis of attitude in the author or in his creation, the watchman, so that we see before us the result of an abstraction, in the aesthetic sense, from a given reality. A constant awareness of this fact will be of assistance to us in the next chapter as we discuss the manner in which this complex of ideas is gradually unfolded and presented to the reader structurally.

IV. THE MANNER OF PRESENTATION

1. There is a difference between a work of art and a manifesto, although sometimes the former can have something of the effect of the latter. But a manifesto presents a position by pressing in a straight line, arguing and deducing, striving for the greatest possible clarity and conviction. The form of an art work is contoured; it grows out of itself and around its own core like a living organism, it is likely to contain ambiguities which reflect the uncertain nature of the reality reproduced in it, and its intellectual skeleton will be thoroughly encased in the luxuriant flesh of its language. Nevertheless, the total effect of the *Gehalt,* woven as it is into the texture of the work and revealed rhythmically by the artist, may come upon us finally with the same strong effect as that of a closely reasoned argument. Such is the case with the *Nachtwachen.* For although I am of the opinion that the primary raison d'être of the *Nachtwachen* is the presentation of its *Gehalt* (which may or may not be regarded as an artistic weakness), still it is presented with artistic acumen, not discursively, but by means of the structure of the work.

Even the casual reader will notice that the purpose of the watchman is to unmask the world and reveal the reality which lies behind surface illusion; the motif of the "Maske" or "Larve" is so pervasive throughout the *Nachtwachen* that it can hardly fail to impress one upon a first reading. Consequently it is fitting that the form of the work should develop in much the same way, progessively revealing to us the attitude of the watchman, requiring us continually to abandon a view of the watchman which we have discovered at various levels to reach finally the core of meaning, somewhat in the way one peels an onion (a metaphor which Bonaventura himself uses: IX, 153-154). As with an onion, however, there is at last no core; at the end of the process of peeling one is left with nothing at all.

To show how this is done, however, it is difficult to keep the totality of the work constantly in view. Much of the complexity of the *Nachtwachen* is due to the fact that it is composed of a mosaic of tiny pieces, a fact which has undoubtedly done much to contribute to the general view that it lacks aesthetic unity. There is little epic cohesiveness in the *Stoff,* and, which the possible exception of the span between X and XIV, not a great deal of dramatic tension in the work taken as a whole. As a matter of fact, though it has been customary to refer to the *Nachtwachen* as a "Roman", it possesses few of the characteristics which we normally assign to that genre, and it seems very largely to elude the categories epic, dramatic, and lyric, thus perhaps confirming our contention that its principle feature is the presentation of *Gehalt*.[1] Because of the atomistic nature of its elements, it is hardly feasible to proceed with our detailed examination of the structure in one clear, connected statement. It will therefore be useful to approach an estimate of the structure obliquely by discussing individually three separate aspects of its form. We shall therefore examine the patterning of motifs, the dissolution of the ground of satire, and finally the manner in which the nihilistic attitude expressed in the work is gradually shown to be the watchman's own.

2. Franz Schultz has already called attention to the presence of

---

[1] Sölle-Nipperdey, p. 83, n. 2, calls attention to the difficulty of classifying the work as "Roman" without, it seems to me, satisfactorily coping with the problem. It is, to be sure, true that one of the features of Romantic prose is the dissolution, or perhaps the greatly increased complexity, of the external novel form. The difficulty, however, lies not so much here as in the predominantly reflective and indeed cerebral tone of the book. One is accustomed to expect of epic that it recreate a self-contained, functioning world of people and events. It could certainly be shown convincingly that the *Nachtwachen* does not do this. Although it is a "Prosawerk mittlerer Länge", one rebels instinctively against classifying it as a *Novelle.*

constantly repeating motifs in the *Nachtwachen,* a fact which he uses as further evidence of the putative carelessness and even lack of memory on the part of the author who is ordering his materials.[2] Once again we are obliged to regard the matter with a more sympathetic eye. There are over a dozen individual motifs which occur repeatedly throughout the book, inviting us to investigate them as a device for unity of construction. Without attempting to order categories or exhaust the possibilities, we can make a list here of the major motifs: the mask, the storm, nothingness, immortality, the Devil, fools (perhaps more accurately connoted by the German word *Narren*), the statue, laughter, night, the poet and literature, the marionette, nature, the world as a stage, and the world of classical antiquity. Of the fourteen motifs here noted, the first ten occur in the first two night-watches, and all have appeared by the end of IV, showing again the extent to which the cycle of I-V already contains the basic elements of the whole work. Some of these motifs exhibit a very considerable pervasiveness; according to my count, the mask and related concepts, for example, occur some twenty-six times, the Devil seventeen, "Narren" eighteen. These figures are significant for a work of such brevity.

To deal with all the motifs of the *Nachtwachen* exhaustively would be rewarding, but it would lead to a stylistic examination in depth which is beyond the scope of this study. However, it is necessary for us to see the way in which these devices are used and particularly how they interrelate to form a fabric of meaning at the symbolic level which gradually takes shape before our eyes. To do this it makes very little difference how we begin; we may select nearly any one of these motifs at random and take note of the various contexts in which it appears. Let us then begin with the Devil. We meet this worthy in the first night-watch, in the person of the priest who is attempting to induce the dying freethinker to a death-bed repentance (I, 6-7). It is a matter of a subtle transformation which takes place before the eyes of the observing watchman. The priest, having had no success with his evocation of damnation, has begun to fulminate in the character

[2] Schultz, *Verfasser,* pp. 132-134.

of the Devil himself, and he is so successful in this that in the eyes of the watchman he begins to appear as the Devil in person, a pretended illusion which goes so far as to induce the satirical watchman to challenge him as such on the street. This apparent dissolution of one character (in this case, a holy man) into his exact opposite (i.e., a demon), is typical for the *Nachtwachen* and at the same time indicative of its frequent subtlety of presentation. The priest, by pretending to be what he ought not to be, becomes and reveals himself to be what he actually is, namely a sinister and hateful figure. This involved metaphor is given more substance in the subsequent phantasmagoria in which three priests masquerade as devils and attempt to kidnap the atheist's body (II, 15-23), all of which culminates in an extraordinarily amusing satire upon the superstition fostered and maintained by the Church (III, 25-27).

At the same time, the motif of the storm is inserted as a background to the devilish struggle for the atheist's body. (The German word *Sturm,* it must be said, refers specifically to a high wind; in the *Nachtwachen* lightning bolts are also a part of the motif. Nowhere does an actual rainstorm or the like occur in the book.) The blazes of lightning and gusts of wind in the lowering sky present, primarily, a visual background of moderate terror for the events. The eerie storm atmosphere, which curiously enough seems to occur high in the heavens without affecting the weather below, has already appeared in I on the very first page, where it reinforces the night atmosphere, and a few paragraphs later (I, 6-7), where it represents the passing of the angel of death at the moment when the atheist expires. The storm motif appears several times subsequently as a background to events of a demonic nature: upon the woodcut which shows the old shoemaker digging for his "treasure" (IV, 46), where it also accentuates the atmosphere of night; in the watchman's ironic and for us weirdly prophetic speculations about the future possibility of man controlling nature (VIII, 137); with increasing intensity in the terrible night in which Ophelia and the child die, where the watchman loses the possibility of more humane alternatives (XIV, 249, 253), and finally, as one would expect, in the graveyard scene, where it not only contributes to the atmosphere, but also provides a specific introduction to the incompetent poet of that scene, leading into the dream-poem on immortality (XVI, 275-277).

We can see that the storm is the intense aspect of the night, which is in turn of course the environment of the *Nachtwachen*. As Helmut Müller observes,

Die Nacht ist die zugleich beglückende und beunruhigende Entdeckung der Romantik – beglückend in ihrem Reichtum, beunruhigend in ihrer Dunkelheit. Sie ist der Schatten des Tages und damit der Schatten des Lebens, von nicht geringerer Wirklichkeit als das Licht und von der gleichen Lebensfülle.[3]

For the *Nachtwachen* particularly, however, the night is the environment in which the truth can be told. This, like so much else in the book, is not revealed at once. The night in the first chapter is merely "eine von jenen unheimlichen Nächten" (I, 1); we are given the atmosphere of one particular night which does not predicate an existential quality to night itself. In the following chapter night even represents a respite from the more active eeriness of the storm: "Die Blitze wurden sparsamer und es blieb längere Zeit Nacht" (II, 22). In IV it is specifically midnight, the "witching hour", the exact antipode of the "Panic terror" of high noon, in which time seems to freeze and the Spaniard is unable to carry out his suicide attempt (IV, 56). In the tale of Don Ponce and Don Juan, however, night itself is presented as possessing innate attributes; it is the only environment suitable to the criminal psychosis developing in Don Juan: "Juan haßte den Tag, und lebte von jezt an nur in der Nacht, denn was in ihm vorging war lichtscheu und gefährlich" (V, 88). It must be remembered that this is the retelling of the Spaniard's story in the "daytime style", in the "klare langweilige Prosa" of the day-dwellers, and thus the night may suitably appear from that assumed point of view as a negative area. The essentially *veridical* quality of the night does not appear explicitly until VII, where the watchman selects the night to relate his own biography precisely for that reason: "Schmeicheln werde ich nicht, denn ich male in der Nacht,

[3] *Die Nachtwachen des Bonaventura*, ed. Helmut Müller (= *Goldmanns gelbe Taschenbücher*, No. 627) (Munich, 1960), p. 5.

wo ich die gleissenden Farben nicht anwenden kann und nur auf starke Schatten und Drucker mich einschränken muß" (VII, 113). Thus we come at last to the true function of the night for this work: its monochromatic barrenness, free from the illusory coloration and richness of the daytime world, is the atmosphere in which the stark truth can be told, in which reality can be effectively demasked. The deadly cold winter night of X and the night of the spring equinox in XIII, wherein man is so unfavorably compared with the life of nature, are now to be seen under this aspect. In the introduction to XVI it would appear that a certain obscurity is the result of the lack of coloration which the telling of night-truth demands:

Ich wünschte dieses Ultimatum und Hogarthsche Schwanzstück meiner Nachtwachen, recht deutlich vor Jedermanns Augen ausmahlen zu können; leider aber fehlen mir die Farben in der Nacht dazu, und ich kann nichts als Schatten und und luftige Nebelbilder vor dem Glase meiner magischen Laterne hinfliehen lassen. (XVI, 272)

But the night does not obscure what would be clearer and more truthful in the daytime; the subjunctive which begins the sentence suggests that it is not possible to relate these events meaningfully at any other time.

In XVI, we will remember, the storm motif has carried us into the area of the poet and literature. This connection is also rooted early in the work. In the second night-watch we are provided with a vignette of the town poet, who, in *Sturm-und-Drang* fashion, gazes out at the storm in the heavens as an analogue to the inner storm of the creative process within him (II, 13), a storm, incidentally, which is liable to be deceptive, since the poetic production inspired by it may very well turn out to be flat and childish once put on paper. But now deception is one of the traditional categories of the Devil, and so it happens that the watchman equates this inner storm with "diesem poetischen Teufel in mir" (*ibid.*), which he suppresses by a blast upon his "antipoeticum", his watchman's horn. Thus, having ranged broadly through the entire book, we have finally succeeded in returning to the original subject of the discussion, the Devil-motif. Here we must pause a moment to call attention to what is happening to our analysis. By beginning with a discussion of one motif, we have been led to another and through that to still others; thus we are able to see how these repeated elements refer to and illuminate one another and are woven together in a fabric which contributes to a comprehension of the book – *quod erat demonstrandum*. We could, of course, now pick up our Devil-motif once again and follow one thread after another back and forth through the work, but this would be wearisome to the reader and highly repetitious, because we would find ourselves returning again and again to the same facts of the *Gehalt* which we have already discussed at some length in this study, since the motifs consistently serve to develop the main themes. We cannot, however, drop the subject of individual motifs without touching upon the high points of the results which such an examination of the motif-pattern would yield.

The vicissitudes of the Devil-motif serve to illustrate what might be called the tendency toward studied ambiguity in the *Nacht-wachen*. In this regard the motif reflects a certain ambiguity inherent in the Christian tradition, wherein the Devil is at once the abhorred source of evil and a necessary counterpoise in the divine scheme of justice. For Bonaventura the Devil represents both the aura of evil which broods over his chaotic universe and an instrument for the revelation of stark truth. That these two functions are not necessarily in contradiction illustrates what can fairly be called the radical pessimism of the work. We have seen how the Devil is a symbol for evil in the opening night-watches. But when the watchman wishes he were the Devil in order to be able to deliver an even more scathing indictment on the night of his "Last Judgment" (VI, 103), or calls forth a vision of the Devil hovering over the world and laughing at mankind stripped of its various cosmetic disguises (XII, 215-216), or asserts that the Devil has invented laughter to lay bare the contemptible core of the world (XV, 260), we begin to feel that the Devil is a repre-sentative of truth in opposition to the deception which God has perpetrated upon the world. These uses of the Devil-motif, in turn, give depth to the watchman's allegorical family relationship with the Devil, presented once as speculation (VII, 112), and once as part of the "gefährlicher psychologischer Schlüssel" which determines his personality (XVI, 279-280). His satirical vocation is devilish both as a source of misery and pessimism, and as an ineluctable urge to reveal truth.

The reference above to laughter calls attention to another motif which has more than one facet. The first extensive exploitation of the motif occurs in IV, where the Spaniard tells the watchman his tragic story only on condition that the latter will laugh at it; because of the terms in which Bonaventura's world is constructed, tragedy has lost its depth, and the presence of Hanswurst in the marionette play, where he succeeds in converting tragedy to farce, reflects a conviction of the impossibility of tragedy in the larger world of living marionettes (IV, 62-63, 65, 67, 69). At the same time laughter begins to take on something of the characteristics of a defense mechanism, in that it becomes a desperate means of maintaining one's identity in the face of the chaos of the world:

Wo giebt es überhaupt ein wirksameres Mittel jedem Hohne der Welt und selbst dem Schicksale Troz zu bieten, als das Lachen? . . . Was beim Teufel, ist auch diese ganze Erde, nebst ihrem empfindsamen Begleiter dem Monde, anders werth als sie auszulachen. (XV, 260)

In other words, by making use of the defense of laughter, one can, as it were, put himself on the side of the Devil and thus avoid the danger of falling victim to illusion. It is a source of preservative strength, and it reminds us strongly of the gypsy's woman's dictum, "Es ist größer die Welt zu hassen, als sie zu lieben; wer liebt begehrt, wer haßt, is sich selbst genug, und bedarf nichts weiter als seinen Haß in der Brust und keinen dritten!" by means of which the watchman recognizes his family relationship to her (XVI, 282). But there is a bitter hollowness in this last of all possible assertions before the advent of madness, especially when viewed against the background of the watchman's hesitating but urgent attempt to discover an alternative in his love-relationship. By getting a glimpse of the fact that this defense is not fully effective, we acquire a sense of the total hopelessness of the human condition in the terms in which Bonaventura presents it.

The motifs of the marionette, the mask, and the world as a stage all belong within the same basic complex of ideas. The marionette, which we have had occasion to mention several times before, has had a considerable history in European literature as a symbol for the problem of free will;[4] here it underlines the meaninglessness of life. The mask illustrates the deceptiveness of outward appearance, and the world as a stage the fraudulence of action. These motifs, which dominate the work as no others do, are at bottom not ambiguous; their ubiquity, however, and particularly the universal application of the mask-motif, serve to show that the work is not a superficial diatribe against willful dissimulation on the part of ill-intentioned persons, but expresses a deep-seated suspicion of the coherence of all external reality. Beneath the mask of life, as becomes increasingly apparent, lies the expressionless skull of death (VIII, 139, 150; XIV, 241; XVI, 295-296); beyond the marionette the conception of man's helplessness in an impenetrable cause-and-effect relationship "so fort bis ins Geheimnißvolle, wo das Regiment nicht mehr zu bestimmen ist" (XV, 265); in the image of the world as a stage, which the watchman has borrowed, one suspects, directly from Shakespeare,[5] a thorough distrust of the substance of human behavior (e.g., VIII, 149). These motifs, by means of their very repetitiveness, mutually illuminate each other and urge upon the reader the deadly seriousness of their import. It does not seem to me correct to regard each occurrence of these motifs as an isolated repetition of the same satirical perspective, as some critics have done; each succeeding occurrence rather gives the total complex greater weight.

Thus far we have been dealing with individual motifs and their relation to one another. To show the extent to which materials are integrated in the *Nachtwachen*, we may now turn to a cluster of several motifs which, for want of a better word, can be gathered together under the heading "petrifaction". Its most elementary

[4] For an interesting review of this matter, see Eleonore Rapp, *Die Marionette in der deutschen Dichtung vom Sturm and Drang bis zur Romantik* (Leipzig, 1924), where it is shown that Bonaventura's use of the motif is the most unrelievedly radical rejection of the doctrine of free will.

[5] *As You Like it*, II, 7

form is the symbol of the statue, which Erich Frank used as a part
of his argument to assign the *Nachtwachen* to Brentano, in whose
works the statue also has symbolic value.[6] Whatever the merits of
Frank's thesis may be, it cannot be denied that he has identified
here a significant element in the text. We first run across the
symbol in the third night-watch, where the watchman begins to
carry out his plan to confound the adulterers. Standing motionless
before a statue of St. Crispin, appropriately enough the patron
saint of shoemakers, he overhears the conversation of the couple,
and when the young man swears that his love stands as firm as
the statue, the watchman puckishly shifts his weight, without,
however, putting the sinners out of countenance (III, 28-30). The
situation of a person masquerading as a statue, or speaking from
behind one, is not infrequent as a folklore motif,[7] and functions
here mainly as a comic element. But there are certain ironies
present which will fit into the general pattern of petrifaction
motifs. The young man, whose love is illicit and apparently only
sexual, compares it to what seems to be a lifeness thing; when,
however, this seemingly lifeless object nevertheless belies his
protestations, he is able to shrug the matter off, testifying in both
ways to the insincerity and unreality of his love. Perhaps it might
be argued that Bonaventura attempts to inject a note of terror
into the scene by the specific reference to the avenging statue in
Mozart's *Don Giovanni* (III, 30). If so, the motif is rather badly
integrated into the scene, since the situation is hardly that serious.
We observe however that the notion occurs to the young man
because he had attended a performance of the opera that evening;
it is very likely that this trivialization of the motif is meant to
point up the shallow frivolity of this character. We are reminded
somewhat of the misuse of Mozart's genius which appears twice
in the work in almost identical words; beginning the marionette
play: "Zuerst giebt es eine Mozartsche Symphonie von schlechten
Dorfmusikanten exekutirt" (IV, 62), and describing the dead poet:
"Drollig bleibt es allerdings, daß du als eine Mozartsche Stimme

---

[6] Frank, *Nw*, pp. xlvi-lii.
[7] For references to this motif, see Stith Thompson, *Motif-Index of Folk-
Literature,* 2d edn. (Bloomington, Indiana, 1955-58), VI, 746.

in ein schlechtes Dorfkonzert mit eingelegt bist' (VIII, 135); in all three cases significant dissonances of life are implied in the allusions. Although *Don Giovanni* is mentioned in one other place (II, 15), and the mysterious Spaniard is named Don Juan, I cannot find that Mozart's opera is in any important way a functional motif in the *Nachtwachen*.

We see statues again in two episodes of what might be called *Schauerromantik*: The Spaniard who fails at his suicide attempt in the courtyard of the cathedral is surrounded by "steinerne Ritter und Heilige" (IV, 56), and "steinerne Jungfrauen", illuminated by candlelight, are mentioned in the scene in which the nun is buried alive (X, 185). Of course, in both cases we identify these things as ordinary stage-props used to generate atmosphere tn the scene, but a rather fine distinction must be made here. The function of the statues is not, as one might expect, to produce terror in the beholder, namely the watchman (an artificial terror, incidentally, since it would be dispelled by daylight), but they are rather a truly symbolic integral part of their respective scenes. The two scenes deal with death from different points of view: in IV, death is sought as a release, but cannot be achieved; in X, it is inflicted as an act of barbarous cruelty. In both scenes demonic and negative forces are at work, forces which destroy the richness and fullness of life. We have already had occasion to mention the scene in XIII in which the mutilated statues of ancient gods and goddesses seem to move threateningly (see above, pp. 52-54). The statues are here remnants of something which has died; they are relics of a living piety of another age which can no longer be revived. Perhaps their illusion of movement at the end of the scene terrifies the watchman for just this reason; they symbolize a category of meaningfulness irretrievably lost and irrelevant to the condition of modern man. The real threat they imply for the consciousness of modern man is forcefully presented by the warning that the sculptured Venus "zu einer eisernen [Jungfrau] ... werden würde" if it had arms (XIII, 223), a reference to the notorious "Spanish maiden" of the medieval torture chamber.

To dispose of the statue-motif in the *Nachtwachen* as a symbol of death would be an oversimplification, however. It would be more accurate to say that it is a symbol of lifelessness; that is, it shows us death where we expect or believe life to be. Thus, in XIII, insofar as the chapter is satirical, its satire is partly directed against the contemporary reverence for classical antiquity which plays such an important role in the eighteenth century, for in Bonaventura's world this esoteric, intellectualized approach to forms which were once symbols of naive, spontaneous piety is absurd in the extreme. So the statue is in a sense a symbol of anti-life, in the same sense in which Werner Kohlschmidt refers to the nihilism of the Romantics as "Anti-Existenz" (see above, p. 70 and n. 6). This will become apparent as we pursue the wider applications of the motif of petrifaction. In the first night-watch the watchman thinks of the silent city of his nightly rounds as a fairy-tale place under a charm, "wo eine böse Macht jedes lebende Wesen in Stein verwandelt hatte" (I, 2). We observe here three things: first, it is a "böse Macht" which is responsible for the lifelessness of the city; second, we are aware of the fact that this city petrified at night is the chief environment of the *Nachtwachen,* thus bringing the motif into meaningful contact with the night-motif; third, the reference to the absence of life is specific (the German word *ausgestorben,* referring to an abandoned place, catches the point more perfectly than any English equivalent, although Bonaventura quite surprisingly does not use it). In the fifth night-watch, where the Spaniard's tale is presented for the second time, we are told, when Don Juan enters Ines' room: "... sie erkannte ihn rasch, und die weiße Rose blühete zum erstenmale roth und glühend auf, und die Liebe belebte Pygmalions kaltes Wunderbild" (V, 86-87). Now the white rose is a symbol of death; it appears later in "Der Traum der Liebe", and immediately afterward in connection with the abandoned bride who has died of a broken heart (X, 178-180); earlier Ines' pallor has been described this way: "... wie eine weiße Lilie blühete eine zauberische weibliche Gestalt . . ., ihre Wangen schienen ohne Leben und die kaum gefärbten Lippen waren still geschlossen; so glich sie mehr dem bedeutungsvollen Bilde eines wunderbaren übermenschlichen Wesens, als einem irdischen Weibe" (V, 82). Thus Ines lacks life, like Pygmalion's statue, until her love for

Juan infuses her with it. In the end, however, just before Juan arranges her murder, "Da lag die Blasse wieder wie an dem Sarkophage" (V, 89), that is, like the stone sculptures found on medieval sarcophagi which represent the dead person within. Again we see the function of the motif; the life which ought to be present in Ines is not there.

In the chill winter night of X the watchman speaks of the "versteinerte Stümpfe" of nature (X, 175); the frozen beggar of this scene, whose death has been caused by the watchman's inaction, is referred to as a statue: "Da ist das Gesicht schon starr und kalt, und der Schlaf hat die Bildsäule seinem Bruder [dem Tod] in die Arme gelegt" (X, 177). This image is immediately followed by the watchman's momentary doubt about his willful negligence; the reasoning here, translated into conceptual terms, is as follows: perhaps indeed the beggar had a right to life and should not have been transformed into a statue, for he wears a lock of his wife's hair and thus carries with him a memory of life and love. But here follows the passage entitled "Der Traum der Liebe", in which love is presented as a momentary delusion without the power to sustain life; so the petrifaction of the beggar was fitting after all. When we endeavor to reproduce Bonaventura's meaning in this fashion, line by line, we begin to acquire some appreciation of the compression he attains with these motifs.

In the final night-watch, the motif of petrifaction is twice used in connection with the watchman's father, once symbolically, with reference to the headstone over his grave: "der ernste steinerne Kopf der Alchymisten blickte mich starr an" (XVI, 279); and once metaphorically, describing the state of his body: "es war noch die abgeformte Büste vom Leben, die hier in dem unterirdischen Museum des Todes zur Seltenheit aufbewahrt wurde, und der alte Schwarzkünstler schien dem Nichts Troz bieten zu wollen" (XVI, 292). The very attentive reader might possibly be startled here, for whereas the motif of petrifaction has heretofore had a consistently negative content, namely lifelessness, it seems here to suggest a positive content, symbolizing resistance to the forces of decay and decomposition which otherwise characterize Bonaventura's universe. But with the sudden disintegration of the alchemist's body we see that the consistency is maintained; the motif of petrifaction refers to the merely lifeless state of the alchemist, and it points ahead to the final disappointment of the watchman when he discovers that no positive existential value whatever can be assigned to the state of his father's body.

It is possible to move from the specific range of the petrifaction-motif into a somewhat wider area of images. Twice, in the quotations above, we have seen the word "starr" (X, 177; XVI, 279). It is a word which understandably occurs frequently in the *Nachtwachen*.[8] We read, for example, of the dead atheist "mit seinem blassen starren Gesichte" (II, 22); of the "Starrsucht" of the Spaniard (IV, 57); of the two brothers who lived together "wie zwei erstarrte Todte auf dem Bernhard Brust gegen Brust gelehnt" (V, 80), and so on. That this paralysis is a symptom of the lifelessness mentioned above is clearly apparent; it is a kind of rigor mortis. A similar idea operates in the description of the lifeless cuckold of III: ". . . alles Leidenschaftliche und Theil-nehmende war auf der kalten hölzernen Stirne ausgelöscht, und die Marionette saß, leblos aufgerichtet, in dem Aktensarge voll Bücherwümer" (III, 31), except that here the character is wooden rather than petrified; the image is reinforced by the wax bust on the man's desk, "als wäre es an einem leblosen Exemplare nicht genug, und eine Doublette nöthig, um die todte Seltenheit von zwei verschiedenen Seiten zu zeigen" (III, 32). The absence of life in this character is very pointedly stressed. Moreover, we observe that we have come back to the marionette-motif; that the latter is intimately related to the petrifaction cluster requires no argument. Both exhibit plainly the lifelessness and delusion of the world as Bonaventura constructs it.

The amount of integration of these materials strikes me as very considerable. The events of the *Nachtwachen* are to a large extent causally unconnected; each operates more or less independently of the other. The constantly recurring images and their inter-

---

[8] The root *starr-* occurs in the *Nachtwachen* twenty-two times, according to Karl Hofmann, "Zur Verfasserfrage der Nachtwachen von Bonaventura" (diss. Prague, [1921]), Table A, a fact worth knowing though quite irrelevant to Hofmann's thesis.

connected patterns are important in the structure of the work as a part of the process of unveiling the inner meaning of these events; by reiterating them constantly, and by weaving them into a consistent pattern which transcends the succession of individual anecdotes, the author forms his total *Gehalt* out of the content of these disparate elements. It is difficult to avoid the conclusion that also in this aspect of the *Nachtwachen* a skillful formative hand is at work.

3. The view of satire prevalent in the Classical-Romantic period and valid enough, it seems to me, for our own day, was succinctly expressed by Schiller:

In der Satire wird die Wirklichkeit als Mangel dem Ideale als der höchsten Realität gegenübergestellt.... Die Wirklichkeit ist also hier ein notwendiges Objekt der Abneigung; aber, worauf hier alles ankommt, diese Abneigung selbst muß wieder notwendig aus dem entgegenstehenden Ideale entspringen.[9]

We have said several times that the watchman's apparent satire turns out to be something much more profound; on the other hand, however, it cannot be denied that there is satire in the work, and in very great abundance. But how is this possible if the watchman has basically no ideal affirmative base from which to operate, as the definition above seems to require? Or, to state the problem another way, if we claim satire as a mode of expression for the work, we presuppose the existence of such an affirmative base, while on the other hand we deny the existence of any such thing for the work as a whole. We can, however, resolve this apparent contradiction in our interpretation, for we shall be able to show with relative ease that the affirmative positions necessary for satirical statement are assumed only provisionally, for that purpose, and that in the subsequent development they are dissolved in the acid of the watchman's *Weltanschauung*. In other words, affirmative statement is only used as a stick with which to beat some other aspect of the world, but it has no permanence upon the shifting ground of the watchman's chaotic universe. We shall

---

[9] Schiller, *Sämtliche Werke,* ed. Gerhard Fricke and Herbert G. Göpfert (Munich, 1958-59), V, 722.

see in this process another way in which the author gradually and obliquely unfolds the purport of his work.

As usual, a prime example for this procedure can be found in the opening section of the work. The first paragraph is notable for its apparent harmlessness:

Die Nachtstunde schlug; ich hüllte mich in meine abenteuerliche Vermummung, nahm die Pike und das Horn zur Hand, ging in die Finsterniß hinaus und rief die Stunde ab, nachdem ich mich durch ein Kreuz gegen die bösen Geister geschützt hatte. (I, 1)

The watchman's simple introductory action of crossing himself evokes what might be called a "stock response" on the part of the reader; he immediately settles down in expectation of an atmosphere of naive piety, naive because of the superstitious fear of evil spirits, piety because of the automatic ritual gesture. The reader finds himself placed in a category of setting which he immediately recognizes. By the middle of III, however, he has been rudely and firmly jolted out of that category; the superstition abetted by the Church has been uproariously satirized and there is no trace of piety left in the atmosphere because the men of the Church have been unveiled not only as fraudulent but also as hateful and, worst of all, ridiculous. The original pretense to piety is, to be sure, not used as a base for satire; it is merely a bit of a joke on the reader, but it illustrates how an apparently firm position can be violently abandoned at a subsequent stage in the action. However, the subsequent position assumed here, that of satire against the Church, does have such a base; it is the watchman's apparent sympathy with the dying free-thinker. Nothing is said which beclouds our image of his strength of character in rejecting, or rather, ignoring, the priest's blandishments at his last hour; he appears as a thoroughly positive figure. We thus find ourselves in the odd situation of having begun the chapter with an apparent gesture of traditional piety and ended it with an affirmation of the dignity of courageous atheism. But this affirmation is not permitted to remain untarnished before we reach the end of the book, because one remark subsequently destroys it as a general value: after the watchman has staged his false Last Judgment, he hears "auch ganz deutlich, wie einige junge Freigeister, welche jezt Synonyma mit Geistlosen sind, keklich behaupteten, daß das Ganze nur ein falscher Lerm gewesen" (VII, 106-107). The fact that the "junge Freigeister" happen to be correct in this case does not alter the caustic effect of this remark. Furthermore, the values which the watchman attempts to assign to the stubborn atheism of his father in the last chapter dissolve into total meaninglessness as his father's body, the symbol of his Promethean opposition, crumbles into dust (XVI, 295-296). Even negative values cannot stand up in the face of the chaos of the universe.

The scene of the dying atheist is, moreover, the beginning of the game of total ambivalence which the watchman plays with the idea of immortality. Here too a hesitant affirmation is apparently made; although it is said that the atheist "schaut blaß und ruhig in das leere Nichts" (1, 5), the watchman has a different response to the dying man's strength in the face of death:

Ich war in diesem Augenblicke seiner Fortdauer gewiß; denn nur das endliche Wesen kann den Gedanken der Vernichtung nicht denken, während der unsterbliche Geist nicht vor ihr zittert, der sich, ein freies Wesen, ihr frei opfern kann, wie sich die Indischen Weiber kühn in die Flammen stürzen, und der Vernichtung weihen (I, 8; see also I, 14 and II, 17).

an idea which Bonaventura may have borrowed from Jacobi.[10] The statement could not appear more certain, yet it has subsequently a peculiar fate. On two separate occasions immortality is simply denied: in the tragedy *Der Mensch,* where the poet "eine Unsterblichkeit in sie hineinerfunden hat" (VIII, 151), and in the dream of the "Gedicht über die Unsterblichkeit" (XVI, 275-277), in which the remains of the dead refuse to respond to the Last Judgment which the poet has called forth. So far we have merely the pattern of affirmation and denial which we have seen in the matter of the atheist. But a further elaboration of the matter appears, wherein it is asserted that man is unworthy of immortality: among the accusations of the false Last Judgment ("denn ihr alle . . ., könnt ihr wohl mit Recht auf den Himmel oder die Hölle Anspruch machen? Für jenen seid ihr zu schlecht, für diese

[10] Michel, *Nw,* pp. liv-lv.

zu langweilig!" VI, 105), and in the "Creator's" monologue in the madhouse, where the philosophical argument in favor of immortality in I is to some extent met:

Was soll ich nun mit ihr [der Puppe, d.h., dem Menschen] anfangen? – Hier oben sie in der Ewigkeit mit ihren Possen herumhüpfen lassen? – Das geht bei mir selbst nicht an; denn da sie sich dort unten schon mehr als zuviel langweilt und sich oft vergeblich bemüht in der kurzen Sekunde ihrer Existenz die Zeit sich zu vertreiben, wie müßte sie sich bei mir in der Ewigkeit, vor der ich oft selbst erschrecke, langweilen! Sie ganz und gar zu vernichten thut mir auch leid; denn der Staub träumt doch oft gar so angenehm von der Unsterblichkeit, und meint, eben weil er so etwas träume, müsse es ihm werden. (IX, 163-164)

The idea of the unworthiness of man for eternity appears again in the doomed speculations of the watchman over the body of his father, in which he would be willing to become enthusiastic over the possibility of immortality for certain titanic figures of the *Sturm-und-Drang* type (XVI, 293-295), but this idea suffers the fate of all the rest with the dissolution of the body of his father. Buried in the "Creator's" monologue is, however, a deeper aspect of the matter, the concept of immortality as a hideous threat, because it would imply a permanent extension of the boredom with characterizes life in the meaningless universe.[11] The notion of eternal life as a punishment, contained in the symbol of the Wandering Jew, appears in the tale told by the Spaniard (IV, 71), and an abysmal fear of the possibilities of immortality accompanies the watchman's love affair in the madhouse:

Ja, ich fürchtete wahrlich den Tod der Unsterblichkeit halber – und beim Himmel mit Recht, wenn hinter dieser langweiligen comedie larmoyante noch eine zweite folgen sollte – ich denke es hat damit nichts zu sagen! (XIV, 247)

Indeed, a few pages later we are given a vision of what real immortality in Bonaventura's universe would mean:

---

[11] Werner Kohlschmidt, "Nihilismus der Romantik", *op. cit.*, pp. 164-165, discusses the connection between "Nihilismus", "Langeweile", "Zeitleere" and "Angst", a pattern which also is found in Kierkegaard and which certainly, at least so far as "Langeweile" is concerned, could be traced down to the literature of the present day.

Kein Gegenstand war ringsum aufzufinden, als das große schreckliche Ich, das an sich selbst zehrte, und im Verschlingen stets sich
wiedergebar. Ich sank nicht, denn es war kein Raum mehr, eben so
wenig schien ich emporzuschweben. Die Abwechselung war zugleich
mit der Zeit verschwunden, und es herrschte eine fürchterliche ewig
öde Langeweile. Außer mir, versuchte ich mich zu vernichten – aber
ich blieb und fühlte mich unsterblich! (XIV, 251)

From this vantage point we can now return to the positive
assertion in I and perhaps see in it a hidden horror, for the immortality which seems here to be positively asserted for the atheist
turns out subsequently to have profoundly hellish qualities. This
does not, however, spare us the dilemma that immortality, whatever the implication, is both asserted and denied in the *Nachtwachen*. Here we are obliged to maintain that such assertions or
denials have no real propositional value but are only tools for
the watchman within the larger framework of his presentation.
Thus, on the one hand, depending upon the context, he makes
immortality appear as an arrogant and foolish dream, and on
the other hand as a threat of cosmic proportions. The emotional
impact is the same: gloom, pessimism and fear. It is with the
achievement of this impact that Bonaventura is concerned, not
with specific theological assertion.

The pattern which we have observed here in this most complex
case has a number of simpler analogues. We can observe, for
example, that the ideal base for satire in the Last-Judgment scene
(VI) is justice, for most of the accusations concern the violation
of the principles of justice in the community; but the very root
of justice is struck at in the courtroom scene of VII, where the
differentiation between the dispensation of justice and the performance of crime becomes very largely erased. Although the
watchman, in foiling the adulterers of III, appears to be upholding
the sanctity of marriage, this impression is removed by one of the
most cynical suggestions in the entire work:

Aus ähnlichen Gründe müßte man z.B. gegen Ehebrecher verfahren,
die bloß um den Hausfrieden aufrecht zu erhalten, gegen die Gesetze
verstoßen; der animus ist hier offenbar ein löblicher, und darauf
kommts doch hauptsächlich an. Wie manche Frau würde nicht ihren

Mann zu Tode quälen, wenn nicht ein solcher Hausfreund sich ein-
fände, und aus reiner Moralität zum Schurken würde. (III, 38)

One of the watchman's brief forays into sentimentality occurs
when he takes charge of the child of the "Unbekannter im Mantel":
"Ich nahm den Knaben in die Arme, und das noch träumende
Leben versöhnte mich wieder mit dem erwachten" (X, 190). But it
pales into insignificance in the face of his remark about the
value of procreation as an act of malicious vengeance against
the meaninglessness of life (XIV, 131). All this is again a process
of the unveiling of the watchman's final insights.

If anything stands relatively firm in the midst of this shifting
conceptual chaos, it is the view of the poet and literature. The
unsuccessful poet of the early part of the book is certainly an
alter ego of the watchman and a totally positive figure. The only
named literary figure who is consistently the object of satire is
one of the standard whipping-boys of the Romantics, Kotzebue
(III, 28; IV, 59; XII, 205; XV, 259); and there is one mild stab
at August Wilhelm Schlegel (IX, 167). But the unquestioned
greats of the literary world are alluded to frequently and more
or less with respect: Böhme (I, 14; IV, 47, 48, 50); Hans Sachs
(IV, 46, 50; VII, 117; XII, 213); Aristophanes (IV, 53); Dante
(IV, 54; VIII, 141; IX, 159); Homer (VII, 121); Goethe (IV, 55;
VIII, 149; X, 176; XII, 204 f., 213; XIII, 223); Lessing (XII,
204 f., XIII, 226); Schiller (XII, 204 f., 211);[12] Tieck (XII, 205);
Horace (XIII, 225), and, of course, Shakespeare (II, 15, 19; IV,
53, 60; V, 82; VIII, 137; XII, 208; XIV, 231 ff.; XV, 256;
XVI, 288). The very frequency of these allusions tells us some-
thing about the primarily literary bent of Bonaventura's interests.
Although the slashes at literary incompetence are too numerous
to mention and there is a deep bitterness both in the watchman's
abandonment of the literary profession and in the apparent im-

---

[12] Whether or not the marionette play in IV is intended as a parody of
Schiller's *Braut von Messina*, as has been asserted by Richard M. Meyer,
"Nachtwachen von Bonaventura", *Euphorion*, X (1903), 583, and denied
by Oskar Walzel, [review of Michel], *Deutsche Literaturzeitung*, XXVI
(1905), col. 2865, and by Michel himself, *Nw*, p. xxxiii, I am unable to
decide, although the parallels suggested by Meyer are striking. If it is true,
it would be an exception to the rule of respect for such persons.

possibility of poetry in the world as the author constructs it, nowhere is literature itself really attacked as an empty or meaningless occupation. Although this interesting lapse has some relationship to the existential value of aestheticism claimed by Romanticism and continuing as a persistent literary attitude down to our own day, I do not believe that the work intends primarily to make any such assertion. Rather, this restriction is necessary to prevent the work from being a total absurdity, a possibility in art which did not appear until about a century later. One might say that Bonaventura cannot muster the objective consistency which would require him to turn his nihilism against his own act, namely the writing of this book. It is perhaps more accurate to suggest that the poet performs the only meaningful act possible in the world, namely the unmasking of it. One could not assert that literature thereby acquires a positive, vital value under the conditions of Bonaventura's world, because for the watchman art simply cannot provide the rich substance of existence which the Romantics claimed for it.

4. We established in the last chapter that the watchman's attitudes are completely formed at the time when he begins to narrate his night-watches and that we do not have a development of the watchman's position in the course of the narration. But neither do we have at the beginning of the work a direct statement on the part of the watchman, which would doubtless have destroyed the *Nachtwachen* as a work of art. We have seen how his position is illuminated by the patterning of motifs and the way in which the ground of satire is dissolved into something which is no longer capable of producing pure satire. We must now inquire how the watchman presents himself to the reader as the purveyor of these ideas, and here we shall observe an interesting fact, namely that the watchman only gradually confesses to these attitudes in his own name.

We have by now ranged back and forth through the book for so long and have absorbed to such an extent the deeper insights of the watchman that we must try once again to put ourselves in the place of a first reader in order to understand this phenomenon properly. It will be remembered that throughout the first three night-watches the book presents a relatively harmless exterior; we seem to be dealing with fantastic satire and Romantic apologetics for the world of literature. Only in the marionette play of IV are we introduced to deeply pessimistic attitudes about the meaning of life. What is important to note here is that the presentation is put into the mouth of the Spaniard and not of the watchman. It is the watchman who retells the story in the daytime-style, and although as narrator he does so to show the superior truth of the Spaniard's version, from the point of view of the first reader the watchman is the observer and commentator upon these matters and not their originator, as indeed he has been largely observer up to this point. Furthermore, as regards the total ordering of the narration itself, it is certainly true that the Spaniard's paralysis at the moment of attempted suicide can be interpreted as a recrudescence of the will to live. Indeed, the watchman suppresses his temptation to aid the Spaniard by giving him his quietus on the grounds that the will to live might reassert itself at the moment of death and thus render the watchman's act a crime (IV, 76), indicating, incidentally, a delicacy which is no longer evident later in the scene in which the watchman permits a beggar to freeze to death (X, 176-177).

Now, however, the watchman is able to abandon slightly his function as observer and indulge in a personal confession which gives us some clue to his manner of thinking; he states that he has

es zu einer absoluten Verworrenheit in mir zu bringen gesucht, eben um, wie unser Herrgott, erst ein gutes und vollständiges Chaos zu vollenden, aus welchem sich nachbar gelegentlich, wenn es mir einfiele, eine leidliche Welt zusammen ordnen ließe. (VI, 94)

The rebellion against the unsatisfactory world which God has created is evident here, but there is also a reflection of the *Sturm-und-Drang* attitude of the poet as *creator ex nihilo*; what God hath put asunder, the literary genius will be able to re-form. The reader does not really receive the explicit impression that the watchman totally shares the attitudes of the Spaniard, and the rest of the chapter contains the Last-Judgment scene which appears, on the surface, to be wholly satirical.

More revealing hints are dropped by the watchman's phantastic speculation upon his origin (VII, 111-112), and his youthful "Leichenrede" (VII, 114-116), which we have had occasion to mention before; but the next searching examination of the condition of life and the world is once again quoted from another, this time the town poet. This passage, including the "Absagebrief an das Leben" and the passages from the tragedy *Der Mensch,* reaches a deeper level than any before; the section begins with the double-entendre "Der Mensch taught nichts, darum streiche ich ihn aus" (VIII, 140), and ends with the symbol of the death's-head as the final mask of the human being (VIII, 152). Still the watchman is largely a spectator, although his comments and observations are increasingly in the spirit of these confessions on the part of others. The same is true of the scene in the madhouse, where, in the midst of all the variegated satire, it is this time the "Creator" who on the one hand expresses the clumsiness inherent in Creation and at the same time symbolizes the incompetent God of Bonaventura's world. But now the watchman is able to insist in his own right upon the conceptual instability of the world:

Ja, wer entscheidet es zuletzt, ob wir Narren hier in dem Irrhause meisterhafter irren, oder die Fakultisten in den Hörsälen? Ob vielleicht nicht gar Irrthum, Wahrheit; Narrheit, Weisheit; Tod, Leben ist – wie man vernünftigerweise es dermalen gerade im Gegentheile nimmt! (IX, 172-173)

As a consequence we note in X that the coldness and joylessness of the presentation has notably increased in intensity; it is here that we have the grisly anecdote of the freezing beggar, the juxtaposition of wedding and funeral, and the burial of the nun in the cloister. Yet again, however, the full expression of nihilism and misanthropy is not given by the watchman, but by the porter at the cloister. After this, however, the watchman is able to reveal himself; the "Lauf durch die Skala", a monologue of emotional dissonance, is touched off by the burial of the nun; feelings are unidentifiable, and the individual personality itself seems to defy location:

Hu! Das ist ja schrecklich einsam hier im Ich, wenn ich euch zuhalte ihr Masken, und ich mich selbst anschauen will – alles ver-

hallender Schall ohne den verschwundenen Ton – nirgends Gegenstand, und ich sehe doch – das ist wohl das Nichts das ich sehe!
(X, 188)

This pronouncement is the turning point for this process in the
Nachtwachen. The watchman has revealed himself as being in
agreement with the position which has previously been taken by
others. It will no longer be necessary to assign the burden of
presentation to others; the watchman himself will now carry the
Gehalt forward. Now, interestingly enough, the function of *satire*
is given to a character other than the watchman, that is, the
character in XII who represents the literary imitativeness and
sterility of the times by wearing Goethe's hat, Lessing's wig and
Schiller's nightcap. By contrast, the watchman's speech in this
chapter is the "Apologie des Lebens", which ends in an assertion
of total materialism. The watchman's letters to Ophelia in XIV
and the two monologues in XV exhibit his position in all its
unrelieved starkness. In XVI, with the final flare-up of an attempt
to read some kind of meaning into the universe, we see a little
more deeply into the watchman's personality, but it is still the
watchman himself with whom we are dealing. It is he who dreams
of the ineffectual Last Judgment; his character which is revealed
down to its base, showing how the dissonances of the universe
have come to a focus in his personality, and his total commitment
to nihilism which crystallizes upon the sudden decay of his father's
body. This is the final perspective from which the world is to be
viewed, a high ground from which we are able to look back and
view the landscape of the whole work.

Thus from the reader's point of view the *Nachtwachen* represents a process of self-revealing on the part of the watchman
which is gradual and carefully controlled in its structural ordering.
If we now call to mind the results of our examination in the first
chapter, we realize that we have a kind of structural counterpoint
in the *Nachtwachen*. There we found as an external form a cyclical
movement boring ever deeper into the empty core of the universe;
here, the convergence of two lines of presentation: the intellectual
content or *Gehalt* and the personality of the watchman. Both the
cyclical process and the process of convergence reach their un-

merciful conclusion in the final night-watch, thus providing the structural dynamics of the work with a clearly definable terminal point.

All three aspects of the *Nachtwachen* treated in this chapter could have been dealt with in much greater detail. Our effort has been to avoid obscuring the larger issue in a mass of detail which would lead us ever again back to the relatively simple issues which form the *Gehalt* of the work. The problem has been to show how the internal structure of the work presents these ideas: we have described a process of gradually revealing the *Gehalt,* illuminating its aspects, demonstrating its consistence, increasingly assigning it to the watchman himself and thus giving it total authority within the framework of the book. That we have been able to do this at such length, with so much of the detail left untouched, is evidence enough that a conscious, skillful hand is at work in the structure of the *Nachtwachen.*

V. THE *NACHTWACHEN* IN ITS TIME

From time to time students of the *Nachtwachen* have attempted to place the work in its literary context by claiming for it certain points of contact with other works in this period. This has been true not only in the narrower endeavor to find parallel passages for the purpose of identifying the author, but also in the larger effort to characterize the work as such. These attempts have been on the whole unimpressive for several reasons. Just as Schultz distorted both the character of the *Nachtwachen* and of Wetzel's works to make his theory appear more plausible, so also are the comparisons of others vitiated by a willingness to accept as significant the lowest common denominator in the *Gehalt* of the two works compared. Moreover, from the very beginning the cart has been before the horse in *Nachtwachen* studies; because there has been a failure in the first instance to understand and appreciate it as a literary text, many of the comparisons made lack a solid base of good judgment. As a result, too much emphasis has been placed on aspects of the work which appear to be derivative, and too little upon its uniqueness and quite unusual freedom from the conventions of the time. This is not to say, however, that the book stands totally isolated; this would hardly be credible. It will be useful, therefore, to examine the literary environment at least briefly to describe more accurately the position of the *Nacht-wachen* in it. We shall be concerned here not only with first-rank phenomena of this greatest of all German literary periods, and the suggestions which scholars have made in that connection, but also with the enormous explosion of popular literature which took place at about the same time. The latter is quite an interesting phenomenon: beginning in the 1770's and extending well into the 1840's there appeared in Germany a "literary" flood the like of which had never been seen before. It began as a trickle in the 'seventies, but

erst in den achtziger Jahren wucherte in den deutschen Gauen, gleich dem geilen Unkraut, eine Literatur empor, deren Ausbreitung und weite Verzweigung bald ins Entsetzliche ging. Das ist jene gemein-schädliche und geistestödtende "schöne Literatur", die blindlings der groben Unterhaltungslust des ungebildeten Haufens fröhnte; das sind die Träber, die das Volk verschlang, während unsere beiden großen Dichter, hoch über der dumpfen Menge stehend, den edlen Feuerwein ihrer Poesie darbrachten.[1]

Some idea of this growth is given by the following figures: in the years 1769-71 some 275 novels appeared at the book fairs in Germany, while the number for the years 1801-03 is estimated at about 1500. The number of professional writers in Germany grew from a little over 3,000 in 1771 to some 12,500 in 1810.[2]

[1] J. W. Appell, *Die Ritter-, Räuber-, und Schauerromantik. Zur Geschichte der deutschen Unterhaltungs-Literatur* (Leipzig, 1859), pp. 1-2. It is difficult to find useful secondary materials on this subject, for obvious reasons, because a meaningful study would require a familiarity with a huge mass of reading which would certainly provide a year or two of misery for the investigator. The volume cited above contains a good many facts and interesting statistics, but fails to characterize the contents of these novels, and Appell is very largely concerned with jingoist rhodomontades against the salaciousness of French literature and with lamenting the harmful effects of such relatively harmless writers as Eugène Sue and Dumas père. Rudolf Bauer, *Der historische Trivialroman in Deutschland im ausgehenden 18. Jahrhundert* (Plauen, 1930), is a sober and scholarly study, but unfortunately it contains nothing of relevance to the *Nachtwachen*. This leaves us with Marianne Thalmann, *Der Trivialroman des 18. Jahrhunderts und der romantische Roman* (Berlin, 1923), a book which, although it is aimed primarily at the importance of the motif of the secret society in the literature of the time, provides an excellent critique and description of the subliterary novel as a whole. My discussion of this aspect of the *Nachtwachen* will be almost exclusively based upon her study. Recently, an amusing and informative study of the novel industry aimed at the German system of commercial lending-libraries has appeared: Walter Nutz, *Der Trivialroman. Seine Formen und seine Hersteller. Ein Beitrag zur Literatursoziologie* (Cologne and Opladen, 1962). Although it deals exclusively with the contemporary situation, I mention it here because the book demonstrates how little the basic conventions and techniques of the genre have changed in over a century and a half.

[2] Figures in Appell, pp. 10-11.

Gottfried Keller at mid-century gave expression to this consuming hunger on the part of the populace for worthless literature in the "Leserfamilie" chapter of *Der grüne Heinrich,* and its seems to have caused much concern generally. Now it must be remembered that Dienemann's *Journal von neuen deutschen Original Romanen,* in which the *Nachtwachen* appeared, at least began as an organ for literature of his quality, although in the last year of its publication (1805) the level of contributions seems to have risen somewhat.[3]

Without any question, certain characteristic motifs, situations and modes of expression which occur again and again in the popular novel have their analogues in the *Nachtwachen.* Before turning to these details, however, one general comment must be made about the subliterary genre, and that is that it is inevitably *plot-centered.* It is concerned with the telling of an involved and intricate story. Complexity of character and vision are completely subordinate to complexity of plot, so that the least possible demand is placed upon the reader; he is simply carried along by the breathless succession of event and adventure. Here already a clear difference from the *Nachtwachen* emerges, for the latter, has, strictly speaking, no plot. Such stories as are told turn essentially upon a single event and are basically anecdotal, with the possible exception of the story of Don Juan and Don Ponce, and the various anecdotes have no cause and effect relation to one another on the level at action. Thus the *Nachtwachen* does not fulfill what seems to be the primary purpose of the trivial novel, namely to serve as entertainment and anesthetic. If we turn now to detail, we can note the following correspondences:

1) The view of landscape in the popular novel is panoramic. Nature is seen from a distance without fastening attention upon particular objects; there is no concentration into symbolic meaning. In general, nature is regarded as friendly, it is refreshing and pleasant. Where it is not friendly; it is portrayed primarily as a hindrance to the action of the story; mountains, for example, are an obstacle to be overcome, not a display of natural majesty

---

[3] See Michel, *Nw,* pp. ix-xii.

in its own right. Both these aspects exhibit a utilitarian view of nature; it is there for man either to relax in or to overcome, and the world is plainly divided into that which is man and that which is non-man, without much symbiosis between the two. In the *Nachtwachen* we find two important confrontations with nature: one in IV and one at the beginning of XIII. Of these, the passage in XIII, the "Dithyrambus über den Frühling", shows the greatest affinity to the above characteristics. It begins with a panoramic view, a valley seen (or rather sensed, since it is night), from a mountainside, and there is no concentration upon objects; indeed, the description is almost totally metaphorical. The passage shows nature at its pleasantest and most benevolent. Moreover, the dichotomy between man and nature is very pronounced; it is in fact the point of the passage. But it is precisely here that the significant difference emerges, for here the dichotomy has become a problem, not because nature provides an impediment to action, but because it raises a question about the very meaning of human existence. Here is nature, calm in its lovely and harmonious cycle of fertility; here is man, disharmonious, ill at ease, separated qualitatively from the rest of Creation. Where does man fit into the otherwise self-sufficient pattern? This is the question raised at this point in the *Nachtwachen*; it is a question quite beyond the scope of the popular novel. Thus nature is not a stage-prop in the *Nachtwachen*; it is an existential problem. As for the description the old shoemaker gives of the young Kreuzgang's sensitivity to the nature around him (IV, 49-50), it belongs, as has been shown above (pp. 61-63), to the sphere of Romanticism; it has no point of contact with the subliterary genre.

2) Among the commonest of individual natural phenomena in the popular novel is the storm. The storm will often have a useful function as a technique of plot construction; at a moment of high crisis, for example, it will cause the travelling hero to seek refuge, thus setting the stage for a fortuitous meeting with a mysterious stranger who will set everything aright. Quite frequently the storm will occur simply to set the mood for events of a frightening and eerie nature. By and large the writer has not integrated the storm into the fabric of his presentation; it is simply

an extraneous stimulus for the reader's mood. We will remember that the storm (in the sense of a high wind) is one of the most frequent motifs in the *Nachtwachen*. In many of its occurrences it has basically much the same function as in the popular novel, providing a fearful backdrop. But eventually the storm acquires symbolic value: "Nahe bei mir heulte noch einer; – doch war es nur der Sturm, der durch das Tollhaus pfiff" (XIV, 253). Here it quite clearly represents the chaos loose in the madhouse of the universe; the storm as a manifestation of nature has acquired meaning and has become integrated into the *Gehalt*.

3) Not unrelated to the function of the storm is that of night in the popular novel. Many of the events in these novels take place at night; frequently they begin (as the *Nachtwachen* does), with the description of an eerie, threatening night-atmosphere. In the night dwells that which is uncommon, dangerous, hard to identify clearly and thus potentially spooky. All this is the most elementary reflection of the irrational but very deep-seated fear of the dark common among children. The night par excellence, as it were, is of course midnight, the "witching hour". In addition to this infantile response, we also find night as the setting for sexual adventure, an important function in view of the preponderance of erotic adventure in the popular novel. So important is the night for the *Nachtwachen* that it will not be out of place to quote here one or two examples from the subliterary presentation. In Karl Grosse's very popular novel *Der Genius* (1791-94), for example, are found the following passages:

Die Schatten der Nacht überraschten uns mit unwillkürlichen Schauder ... die Blätter zitterten mit einem matten Geräusch, wir waren von Phantomen umringt. Unsere Existenz war selbst ein Phantom.[4]

Das junge Laub beugte sich eben so halb durchsichtig in das Dunkel herab und schien von geheimen Schrecken zu beben; ein zarter Luftstrom schauderte bei mir balsamisch vorbei; alles atmete einen Geist gespannter Erwartung und die Schatten glichen schwärmenden Elfen.[5]

Thus the night is an area of fear and phantasy, as in the *Nacht-*

[4] Grosse, *Der Genius*, IV, pt. 1, p. 11, quoted in Thalmann, p. 40, n. 66.
[5] Grosse, *Der Genius*, I, 42, quoted *ibid*.

wachen, a realm of heightened suspense and hidden realities. By
contrast, as in the *Nachtwachen,* the day belongs to the ordinary
reasoning intellect. A real point of contact is not to be denied
here. But in the popular novel the day gains the victory over the
night; much of what takes place in the night is explained and
revealed subsequently in the clear daylight of reason. The atmosphere of the night is not an enduring experience; it is a particular
experience which belongs to the extraordinary events of the novel.
This is one of the phenomena which brings Marianne Thalmann
to her conclusion that the popular novel is basically rationalistic
in outlook, and even its spookiness is merely stage-dressing oper-
ating within an essentially rational universe. Bonaventura turns
this whole outlook upside down. The night retains its terror and
lack of clarity, but for him these things are true; they are a reflection of the basically chaotic, irrational universe which the perspective of daytime serves only to distort. The experience of night
endures; it is not susceptible to a happy ending.

4) A relatively minor matter is the frequency in the popular
novel of stage-props suggesting death. These include the cemetery,
the skull, the open grave (occasionally the scene of erotic adventure), and grisly interment scenes. All these things occur in the
Nachtwachen, but their function goes far beyond the attempt to
give the reader a pleasurable shudder. The skull as the last mask
of death is a symbol of profound dismay (esp. VIII, 139, 152),
and the cemetery locale of XVI is intimately connected with the
logical conclusion of the work. The scene in X in which the nun
is buried alive can perhaps be interpreted as a convention borrowed from the popular novel to generate a feeling of horror,
but the main interest of the scene is focussed not upon the sen-
sational event itself, but upon the watchman's response to it
("Lauf durch die Skala", X, 186-188), and upon the tale of
shattered values told in XI which provides the background for
the scene. The popular novel prefers to cope with death in the
tangible form of murder, battle, and other types of violence and
slaughter; the attitude toward death is one of undifferentiated
fear. Of this approach to death in the popular novel Marianne
Thalmann remarks: "Diese Kunst ist aber für eine Symbolik noch

nicht reif. Sie greift daher ganz überwiegend nach dem Tatsäch-
lichen und lebt ihr Verhältnis zum Tod, zur Vergänglichkeit in
greifbaren Situationen aus".[6] It is fair to say that Bonaventura
has surpassed this limitation.

5) The plot of the trivial novel turns with monotonous predic-
tability upon secret complications in family relationships. Either
the hero grows up in ignorance of his true parentage and heritage,
or he falls in love with a girl who turns out to be his sister, or
some similar confusion provides the machinery for the plot. This
is an ancient fairy-tale motif, older than Oedipus, and has deep
psychological roots. But it provides the hack writer with a technique which is extraordinarily easy to manage. Inexplicable events
can thus be presented to the reader with great complexity and
mystery to form a situation which is totally impenetrable to him
until the author, who has been able to keep these simple facts in
mind throughout, chooses to explain it. It is no doubt this effective
but easy technique which accounts largely for the extraordinary
productivity of some of the writers in this genre.[7] This motif was
by no means confined to the subliterary level; one need only think
of Goethe's *Wilhelm Meisters Lehrjahre,* Tieck's *Franz Sternbald,*
Brentano's *Godwi,* or Schiller's *Braut von Messina* for four examples among many for the pervasiveness of this technique of plot
construction. Now the watchman is also unaware of his true
parentage, and the truth is revealed to him in the dénouement
(if one may apply such a term to a novel without a plot) of the
work. Thus far Bonaventura participates in a literary fashion of
the time, but no farther. In the first place, considerations of plot
and dramatic tension are minor in the *Nachtwachen*; the ignorance
of parentage is not a device in the same sense as it is in the
popular novel. In the second place, the watchman's parentage is
a "gefährlicher psychologischer Schlüssel" (XVI, 281); it explains,
not events, but attitudes; explains causal relationships not on a
rational, realistic level, but on a deeper plane which is both

---

[6] Thalmann, p. 44.

[7] E.g., in fifteen years Spieß succeeded in producing nineteen novels
totalling forty-three volumes (Appell, p. 40). Modern writers, through the
miracle of the typewriter, frequently do much better. For some staggering
figures, see Nutz, *Der Trivialroman, op. cit.,* pp. 86-87.

allegorical and existential. The watchman's descent from the wild gypsy woman and the atheistic black magician, with the Devil standing godfather, is a many-faceted symbol which reflects light backward over the whole novel. Thus Bonaventura has probed more deeply into an idea which must have some meaning in the popular tradition just because of its very ubiquity, and perhaps he is in a sense one of those who came to realize the potentialities hidden in the conventions of the subliterary writers, for, as Marianne Thalmann says of them, "in der Gesamterscheinung dieser Romane bedeuten die alten Motive ein Wollen, das sinngemäß mehr sagen will, als Ausdruckskraft vorhanden ist".[8]

6) A standard figure in the trivial novel is the mysterious stranger who appears at crucial moments in the course of events, usually in possession of all the information necessary to unravel the mystery, and who often presents himself as a magician purporting to exorcise spirits or perform similar feats. True to the rationalistic tendency of the genre, these feats are eventually unmasked as fraud, sometimes with intricate mechanical explanations. This pattern too found its way onto a higher literary plane; Schiller, who apparently was game to try any literary mode then current, presents it in its most pristine form in *Der Geisterseher* (1787-89), although, to be sure, this was one experiment he was to live to regret. The subsequent impact upon E. T. A. Hoffmann is of course obvious. The connection here with the *Nachtwachen* is fairly remote. Although the magician, Kreuzgang's father, is modeled somewhat on this pattern, he is not a motive force in the plot, and indeed we never see him alive. Nor is his ability as an adept given a rationalistic explanation; for the sake of Bonaventura's allegorical purposes the old magician's exorcism of the Devil is left quite unquestioned. To place the "Unbekannter im Mantel" (X, 182) in this context, as Schultz does,[9] is incorrect. There is nothing mysterious about this figure per se; the watchman quite frankly tells us that he has no time to relate his story now, and the connection of the stranger to the events in the cloister is quite satisfactorily explained in the subsequent night-

---

[8] Thalmann, p. 45.
[9] Schultz, *Verfasser,* p. 278.

watch. On the subject of magic, however, it is perhaps of some interest that one of the standard phenomena of exorcism scenes, the magic blue light, which appears in novel after novel, occurs also in the *Nachtwachen* (XVI, 279). In all these cases, it can be seen that the standard situations of the popular novel have considerable influence on the *Nachtwachen*. But we can also see that in the *Nachtwachen* the realm of *Unterhaltungsliteratur* has been left far behind.

It would be of interest to be able to look at the whole series of Dienemann's *Journal* in order to take some measure of the company in which the work appeared. However, most of these works have sunk into deep obscurity. Michel in 1904 was unable to locate all the items,[10] and today it would undoubtedly be even more difficult to put together a complete set. I was able to see two of them: Karl Nicolai's *Franz von Werden*, which encompasses Nos. 3-6 of the 1802 series, and Christian Vulpius' *Don Juan der Wüstling*, No. 2 of the 1805 series. The second of these is of little interest here. Vulpius, who made a career out of being Goethe's brother-in-law, was an indefatigable writer of popular novels and every other kind of saleable literature, and succeeded in producing one of the colossal best-sellers of his time, *Rinaldo Rinaldini* (1798). His *Don Juan,* though it purports to be a translation of Tirso de Molina's drama, lacks both charm and tragic depth, and does not merit further examination. Nicolai's novel is a good deal more respectable; it is an epistolary novel of an impossible love affair, clearly in the wake of Richardson, perhaps by way of Goethe's *Werther*. Nicolai's language is not without grace, and the impact of the clear simplicity and exactness of Goethe's prose style is quite evident. But the novel is hardly of the first rank, or even nearly so; it wades through endless swamps of *Empfindsamkeit,* turns upon uncritical adherence to the virtues of chastity, loyalty, and filial obedience, and has no trace of the depth of personality found in *Werther;* the good characters are incredibly and flawlessly good, and the evil characters unremittingly bad, though some of them achieve repentance. It is without question a dull book. Distinct affinities to the

[10] Michel, *Nw,* pp. ix-x, where a complete list of the contents is given.

subliterary motifs mentioned above are present. There is a mysterious stranger who brings about a climax by staging a fraudulent exorcism. There is a wealth of adventure: dueling, murder, fire, attempted seduction, etc. There are storms at sepulchral moments. The complications of the plot turn on the hidden fact that the lovers are brother and sister. Other motifs of the popular novel, which we have not mentioned because they have no analogue in the *Nachtwachen,* are also present. *Franz von Werden* is a commercial novel fully in the spirit of its age; the fact that there is not the remotest ground in it for comparison, in any important sense, with the *Nachtwachen* helps us to our conclusion concerning the relationship of the *Nachtwachen* to the popular novel. The *Nachtwachen* is certainly indebted to the subliterary mode; one would not hesitate to conclude that the author had done, or could do, such hack writing of his own. But the *Nachtwachen* has a vision and an originality of form which put it quite out of this realm; we cannot, with any claim to plausibility, classify it under this rubric.

What then, about its relations to the world of literature which has survived its time and passed into the canon? A number of literary productions have been suggested as being related in one way or another to the *Nachtwachen.* The best of these suggestions concerns Tieck's *William Lovell* (1793-96).[11] It is not surprising that this gloomy novel, reflecting the emotional distress of Tieck's young manhood, should come to mind upon reading the *Nachtwachen.* We need only listen to some of the characters to see why this should be so; for example, Lovell himself:

Shakespeares Hamlet ist meine tägliche Lektüre, hier finde ich mich wieder, hier ist es gesagt, wie nüchtern, arm und unersprießlich das Leben sei, wie Wahnsinn und Vernunft in einander gehn und sich einander vernichten, wie der nackte Schädel endlich über sich selber grinset und hohnlacht, und von aller Schönheit und Lust, von allem Ernst und aller Affektation nichts mehr als diese weise widerwärtige Kugel übrig bleibt – O meine Phantasie sieht Gestalten![12]

Or Balder:

---

[11] E.g., Sölle-Nipperdey, pp. 25, 70.
[12] Tieck, *Schriften* (Berlin, 1828), VI, 170-171.

Unser ganzes Leben [ist] ein unnützes Treiben und Drängen, das elendste und verächtlichste Possenspiel, ohne Sinn und Bedeutung. . . . Könnt' ich nur Worte finden, um die Verachtung zu bezeichnen, in der mir alles erscheint, was *Mensch* heißt![13]

Similarly, in the posthumous papers of Lovell's father:

Ich habe einen Blick hinab ins Thal des Todes gethan, und nun taumeln alle Wesen dieser Welt nüchtern und leer meinen Augen vorüber. Alles sind nur Larven, die sich einander selbst nicht kennen, wo einer dem andern vorübergeht, und ihm ein hohles Wort giebt, das jener durch ein unverständliches Zeichen beantwortet.[14]

Burton's father has lived his life with much the same view:

So leben wir vielleicht auf einer unterhaltenden abwechselnden Masquerade, auf der sich der am besten gefällt, der am unkenntlichsten bleibt, und lustig ist es, wenn selbst die Maskenhändler, unsere Geistlichen, und unsere Lehrer, von ihren eigenen Larven hintergangen werden.[15]

Such passages could be quoted in considerable numbers, but the four here cited are sufficient to show that *William Lovell* has a familiar ring to one coming directly from the *Nachtwachen*. The loss of faith in the external appearance of life, the view of death as a senseless finality, a contempt for the world in toto, all are expressed in similar terms and symbols.

When we look at the novel more closely, however, we discover some significant differences. They can best be summed up by saying that the *Nachtwachen* is considerably more radical, precisely because of its lack of multiple dimensions; the complexities of Tieck's novel offer extenuating circumstances. The elder Burton, for example, is clearly a man thoroughly evil down to the root of his soul, and thus within the context of the novel his views can be rejected as in any way representing a proper perspective. No moral judgment upon the watchman in terms of good and evil is made anywhere in the *Nachtwachen*; these categories lack content in Bonaventura's universe. The elder Lovell is a man crushed to despair by the pressure of great misfortune; the quota-

---

[13] *Ibid.*, VI, 221, 224.
[14] *Ibid.*, VI, 330.
[15] *Ibid.*, VII, 63.

tion above is not at all characteristic of his general outlook upon life. Though the watchman has his share of adversity and bad luck, it is by no means sufficient to explain his attitudes. Balder is mad, or at least becomes so, and the watchman, despite his repeated pose of "Narr", is not. As for Lovell himself, he is hardly a representative human being. He is a young man of appallingly weak character who ultimately fails to submerge his baser instincts in a welter of rhetoric and shibboleths which he has mistaken for idealism, and so loses faith in something which had no substance to begin with. Moreover, in the last analysis, he is rather stupid, as his seducer takes pains to point out eventually, and the watchman is clearly not stupid; we have already had occasion to observe that it is precisely the sharpness of his intellect which has brought him to this spiritual state. For Tieck, therefore, though he is deeply involved himself in these problems, such attitudes are still aberrational; they are subjected to criticism and balanced off against a more reasonable and decent relationship to life in the characters of young Burton and Mortimer. This, to be sure, does not quite come off, for the counter-picture of virtue is rather dull and philistine; Tieck himself was quite aware of this most significant difficulty, when he excused himself, on the ground of his youth, in the preface to the second edition in 1813:

Dies möge ihn entschuldigen, wenn der Leser finden sollte, daß der Dichter seinem Vorwurf nicht gewachsen war, und besonders jene Gegend, die der Verwirrung, dem Geistesluxus, dem Zweifel, der philosophirenden Sinnlichkeit und Leidenschaft als ein helles Elysium gegen über liegen sollte, nur als dunkle Schattenmasse hingestellt hat.[16]

This early incapacity to provide a plausible contrast to his dark thoughts is ominous, but Tieck succeeded in overcoming it. For the watchman it is permanent. Nonetheless, we cannot deny that the Tieck of *William Lovell* participates to a considerable degree in the world which we find in the *Nachtwachen*.

Another work which is sometimes mentioned is Karl Philipp

[16] *Ibid.*, VI, 5.

Moritz's *Anton Reiser* (1785-90).[17] Here I think we are a little
farther from the mark. True, reading the book is a dark and
gloomy experience; it creates an atmosphere of genuine sadness.
Strictly speaking it is not a novel at all, but a thinly-disguised
autobiography. It contains a most astonishing psychological self-
analysis, absolutely modern in its approach, for it does not
proceed from emotional problems to a misplaced sense of guilt,
but derives them from their true source, the unconscious cruelty
of parents and their allies to children. Though Moritz never succeeded in "curing" himself – despite his very considerable gifts
he remained throughout his life hampered and spiritually emas-
culated by that nightmarish childhood – it would be quite acceptable in terms of psychological theory to suggest that by facing his
problem, discovering its roots, and turning it into a novel, he at
least provided himself with the strength for survival. But this brief
characterization will show how far removed *Anton Reiser* is from
the *Nachtwachen*. Here again we are dealing with aberrations, this
time aberrations which proceed from identifiable sources. Beneath
the surface of *Anton Reiser* lies the conviction that life can be
good and decent, and indeed it is the unfulfilled yearning for such
a life which makes the book so sad. In the *Nachtwachen* there is
no possibility of such an assumption, and thus the two works
operate in totally different contexts.

A somewhat surprising suggestion was made by Korff: he
compares the *Nachtwachen* with Friedrich Maximilian Klinger's
Fausts Leben, Thaten und Höllenfahrt (1791).[18] Klinger's late
novels have been rather forgotten. One reason for this might be
that they are not a factor in the history of literature; they retain
some of the stylistic elements of *Sturm und Drang* (Klinger's own
phrase, of course) nearly twenty years after that movement had
ceased to be a productive vehicle in German literature. But in
strength of language, scenic skill, grandiose and obscene satire,
and sheer entertainment value, Klinger's *Faust* exhibits definite
virtues. In its scenes of the underworld it shows unmistakeably
the impact of Milton, something rather unusual in Germany. In

---

[17] E.g., Sölle-Nipperdey, p. 69.
[18] Korff, *Geist der Goethezeit*, III, 226.

this novel Faust succeeds in philosophizing himself into a position which has some similarity with the watchman's. A dialogue between Faust and Leviathan will illustrate this most clearly:

Faust: Ist der Mensch durch der Notwendigkeit Kette zu handeln gezwungen, so muß man seine Handlungen und Thaten den höchsten Wesen selbst zuschreiben, und sie hören dadurch auf, strafbar zu seyn. Kann von einem vollkommnen Wesen etwas anders als Gutes und Vollkommnes fließen? Nun, so sind es unsere Handlungen, so scheußlich sie uns vorkommen mögen, und wir sind ihr Opfer, ohne abzusehen, warum. Sind sie sträflich und das, was sie uns scheinen, so its dieses Wesen ungerecht gegen uns, denn es straft Greuel an uns, deren Quelle es selbst ist. Teufel! löse mir diese Rätsel, ich will wissen, warum der Gerechte leidet und der Ruchlose belohnt wird?

Teufel: Faust, du hast zwey Fälle gesetzt, wie, gäb' es vielleicht noch einen dritten? Nämlich, daß ihr auf die Erde geworfen wärt, wie Staub und Gewürme, ohne Vorsicht und Unterschied. Einen dunklen Wirrwarr überlassen, den man euch, wie ein verworrenes Knäuel übergeben hätte, ihn auseinander zu zerren; geläng' euch auch das unmögliche Werk nicht, euer strenger Herr und Richter fordert' euch aber doch dafür zur Rechenschaft?[19]

Thus the sense of despair is tied to an ancient problem, namely, the presence of evil in a world governed by a God presumed to be good and just. But Faust has no final answers; in the end Leviathan himself shows Faust how his arrogant interference in the natural order of events has only succeeded in generating more evil than would otherwise have occurred. Thus it is a highly moral book; it is part of a series of novels which Klinger wrote to express what are at bottom quite conventional views of life and the world:

Sie sollten die ganze Fragwürdigkeit dieser so herrlichen wie schrecklichen Wirklichkeit offenbaren und über ihr den Sieg der eingeborenen moralischen Kraft durch ein reines tätiges Wirken des Menschen zeigen. Darin näherte er sich dem autonomen sittlichen Pflicht- und Bildungsgedanken der Klassik.[20]

Once again we are obliged to note that the differences outweigh the similarities. Klinger represents, in the last analysis, strength,

---

[19] Klinger, *Fausts Leben, Thaten und Höllenfahrt*, 2d edn. (Karlsruhe, 1792), pp. 105-106.
[20] Fritz Martini, *Deutsche Literaturgeschichte von den Anfängen bis zur Gegenwart*, 7th edn. (Stuttgart, 1956), p. 209.

optimism, and conventionality; Bonaventura deep despair and near madness.

Jean Paul's influence upon Bonaventura has been noted by just about everyone who has written on the *Nachtwachen*. In fact, Jean Paul himself, who is the only writer of first rank on record as having read the *Nachtwachen* at all, recognizes his own influence; he writes to Thieriot on Jan. 14, 1805:

Lesen Sie doch die Nachtwachen von Bonaventura, d.h. von S<chelling>. Es ist eine treffliche Nachahmung meines Gianozzo, doch mit zu vielen Reminiszenzen und Lizenzen zugleich.[21]

The book is drenched with the influence of Jean Paul: the frequency of learned or pseudo-learned remarks, the semi-lyrical "Standreden", the terminology of the drama, even individual words, phrases and motifs, and much more, are traceable to this model.[22] It is of considerable importance also that Bonaventura, like Jean Paul, refuses to be a camp-follower of either the Classical or the Romantic school, and achieves a position influenced by, but not participating in, either form.

But despite this clear dependence, there are differences here as well. Jean Paul himself compares the *Nachtwachen* to "Des Luftschiffers Gianozzo Seebuch", from the *Komischer Anhang zum Titan* (1801). Here a satanically satirical character hovers far above the world in his airship, excoriating the vices of "Ungerechtigkeit" and "Aufgeblasenheit".[23] It differs from the *Nachtwachen* to the extent that the latter is not basically satire, although acidulous satiric violence is common to both. Frequently mentioned in connection with the *Nachtwachen* is also the curious "Erstes Blumenstück" inserted in *Siebenkäs* (1796-97), "Rede des toten Christus vom Weltgebäude herab, daß kein Gott sei". In this nightmarish scene, the spectre of Christ appears before ghosts

---

[21] Ernst Förster, *Denkwürdigkeiten aus dem Leben von Jean Paul Friedrich Richter* (Munich, 1863), I, 457. The name "Schelling", here suppressed, was restored by Schultz, who located the original MS of the letter (*Verfasser,* pp. 31-32 and n. 3).

[22] An interesting list of such allusions may be found in Michel, *Nw,* pp. xix-xxiii.

[23] Jean Paul, *Sämmtliche Werke,* ed. Ernst Förster, 3d edn. (Berlin, 1860-62), XVII, 104.

of the faithful at midnight to announce that there is no God; throughout the universe he has only been able to find emptiness. The similarity to the hollow universe of the *Nachtwachen* is at once apparent. Jean Paul, who sensed very acutely the cleft soul of modern man, is capable of entertaining this possibility and committing it to literary form. But the passage must be seen in its context. This is not the sum of Jean Paul's wisdom; it is a possibility, or rather, a threat proceeding out of the intellect to one's deeper faith. Jean Paul is capable of thinking the thought, but at the same time he is obliged to deny it. This he makes clear in a footnote at the beginning of the passage:

Wenn einmal mein Herz so unglücklich und ausgestorben wäre, daß in ihm alle Gefühle, die das Dasein Gottes bejahen, zerstöret wären; so würd' ich mich mit diesem meinem Aufsatz erschüttern und – er würde mich heilen und mir meine Gefühle wiedergeben.[24]

Moreover, when we look at the vehicle in which it appeared, the novel *Siebenkäs,* we observe that it is an extraordinarily gentle book. It probes the unhappy lack of communication between two good people, and shows how love can fail to bridge the gap which only widens in the frustrations of everyday events. Kindness and deep humanity speak out of the pages of *Siebenkäs,* an atmosphere far removed from that of the *Nachtwachen.* The world of Jean Paul is as multifarious and complex as his style; Bonaventura's basic attitude is quite simple. Jean Paul is concerned with the gap between the ideal and the real; Bonaventura has lost all contact with the ideal. A recent German dissertation observes:

Die Humoristen Jean Pauls ... verlachen die Welt, da sie unter der Nichtigkeit der Idee im Leben leiden; die Idee als solche bleibt davon jedoch unberührt. In den "Nachtwachen" dagegen wird die Idee selbst mit ins Lächerliche einbezogen, denn der Teufel, der eigentliche Gegenspieler der Idee, hat das Lachen in die Welt geschickt [XV, 260].[25]

Although we have been concerned in this brief sketch of some

---

[24] *Ibid.,* XI,   266.
[25] Heinrich Köster, "Das Phänomen des Lächerlichen in der Dichtung um 1800 (Jean Paul, E. T. A. Hoffmann, Bonaventura)" (diss. Freiburg im Breisgau, [1956]), p. 224.

of the contemporaries of the *Nachtwachen* to show the extent to which it is unique, more radical than its literary environment, we cannot fail to observe that much the same problem is present in all these productions. Whether we consider Lovell's programmatic libertinism, Anton Reiser's deep neurosis, Faust's striving against the divine order, or Jean Paul's capacity to express frightful possibilities which run counter to his instincts, we are merely approaching from different angles one of the most persistent problems of modern man, namely, to achieve meaning, will, and survival in a world in which God is hidden, unknowable, or dead. The abyss which has opened in the last three hundred years between man and God and between man and the universe is identifiable in all these works. It is merely that Bonaventura is concerned *only* with this problem, and, seen in his radical perspective, all other considerations such as morality and humanity, which find a place in the other works, fall into insignificance.

The *Nachtwachen* occupies a lonely place in German literature. It has few significant antecedents, and no direct descendants at all. Although it is symptomatic of crises which were to come to a head in the nineteenth century and which have borne bitter fruit in our own, it is isolated as a work of art. It has been the purpose of this study to attempt an adequate understanding of it, and thus to retrieve it, not as a curiosity, as has been done in the past, but as a work which commands our respect, from beneath the detritus of the centuries which doubtless has buried many an unrecognized literary gem. The *Nachtwachen* may not be a link in the chain of literary history, but it has a rightful place in the treasure-house of the past.

BIBLIOGRAPHY

I. THE EDITIONS IN CHRONOLOGICAL ORDER [1]

Bonaventura, [pseud.], *Nachtwachen. Von Bonaventura* (Penig, 1804 [1805?]).

The original edition appeared as No. 7 of the third year of the *Journal von neuen deutschen Original Romanen,* published by "F. Dienemann und Comp." at Penig in Saxony. The first title page reads: "Dritter Jahrgang. 1804 / Siebente Lieferung. / Nachtwachen." The second title page reads: "Nachtwachen. / Von / Bonaventura. / Penig 1805." This suggests that the publication might have been behind schedule and that the correct date is 1805. However, Jean Paul's letter of Jan. 14, 1805 (see above, p. 118 and n. 21) makes this most unlikely. An advertisement for the *Nachtwachen,* with an excerpt from the book ("Prolog des Hanswursts zu einer Tragödie der Mensch", VIII, 144-152) appeared in the *Zeitung für die elegante Welt,* July 21, 1804 (No. 87), cols. 691-694, with the following note: "Fragment aus einem noch ungedruckten Roman: N a c h t w a c h e n von Bonaventura, der zur Michaelsmesse herauskommen wird" (col. 691). It is therefore likely that the book did appear at the autumn in 1804, and that the second title was post-dated to preserve its newness.

Meissner, Alfred, ed., *N.v.B.* (= *Bibliothek deutscher Curiosa,* Vols. II-III). (Lindau and Leipzig, 1877; Berlin, 1881).

Review: [Scherer, Wilhelm], *Deutsche Rundschau,* XI (1877), 350.

Michel, Hermann, ed., *N.v.B.* (= *Deutsche Literaturdenkmale des 18. und 19. Jahrhunderts,* No. 133) (Berlin, 1904).

Reviews: Michel, Wilhelm, *Allgemeine Zeitung (Beilage),* 1905, No. 206. – Walzel, Oskar, *Deutsche Literaturzeitung,* XXVI (1905), cols. 2862-6. – Walzel, Oskar, "Schriften zur Romantik", *Das literarische Echo,* VIII (1905-06), cols. 574-575.

See also under Michel, Hermann, in Part II of this bibliography.

Schultz Franz, ed., *N.v.B.* (Leipzig, 1909).

See also under Schultz, Franz, in Part II of this bibliography.

[1] "*N.v.B.*" will be understood to refer to the usual title, *(Die) Nachtwachen von Bonaventura*; variant titles will be noted.

Anonymous, ed., *N.v.B.* (Berlin, 1910).

Frank, Erich, ed., *Clemens Brentano. Nachtwachen von Bonaventura* (Heidelberg, 1912).
Reviews: Amelung, Heinz, "Neues und Altes, Echtes und Falsches von Clemens Brentano", *Das literarische Echo*, XV (1912-13), cols. 1114-9. − Berend, Eduard, *Euphorion*, XIX (1912), 796-813. − Cardaunus, H., "Wer war Bonaventura?" *Hochland*, X (1912-13), 751-754. − Friede-mann, T., "Überraschungen von Clemens Brentano", *Hamburger Nachrichten (Literaturblatt)*, 1913, Nos. 43, 44. − Morris, Max, *Deutsche Rundschau*, CLIV (1913), 474. − Schultz, Franz, "Zu den 'Nachtwachen von Bonaventura' ", *Archiv für das Studium der neueren Sprachen und Literaturen*, CXXIX (1912), 12-15. − Schulze, Friedrich, *Literarisches Zentralblatt*, LXV (1914), cols. 554-555.
See also under Frank, Erich, in Part II of this bibliography.

Steinert, Raimund, ed., *N.v.B.* (= *Der Liebhaberbibliothek neunzehnter Band*) (Weimar, 1914).
Subsequent printings are: Weimar, 1916; Weimar, 1917; Potsdam, 1920.

Schultz, Franz, ed., *N.v.B.* (Leipzig, 1919).
Second printing of 1909 edition; reset but otherwise unchanged. (Re-printed Leipzig, 1921.)

Anonymous, ed., *N.v.B.* (= *Die Drucke des Bücherwinkels*, Druck 3) (Munich, [1923]).
Deutsches Bücherverzeichnis for 1921-25 reports: "Mit 17 Orig.-Rad. v. B. Goldschmitt". Bruno Goldschmitt's etchings appear also in Schultz's edition of 1947 (see below). I have not been able to discover whether Schultz was the editor of this edition.

Merbach, Paul Alfred, ed. *N.v.B.* (= *Das Wunderhorn*, No. 8) (Berlin, [1924]).

Anonymous, ed., *N.v.B.* (Berlin, 1925).
Deutsches Bücherverzeichnis for 1926-30 reports: "Mit Original-Lithographien v. Louis [sic] Corinth."

Müller, Andreas, ed., *N.v.B.* (= *Deutsche Literatur in Entwicklungsreihen, Reihe Romantik*, XVI) (Leipzig, 1930), 13-117; 246-251.

Hendriksen, Jørgen, ed., *N.v.B.* (= *Deutsche Texte*, ed. Carl Roos, Vol. III) (Copenhagen, 1943).

Widmer, Walter, ed., *N.v.B.* (Zurich, 1945).

Riemeck, Renate, ed., *N.v.B.* (Wedel, 1946).

Schultz, Franz, ed., *N.v.B.* (Munich, 1947).
"Mit siebzehn Reproduktionen nach Radierungen von Bruno Gold-schmitt" (t.p.). Cf. under anonymous edition of [1923].

Pfeiffer-Belli, Wolfgang, ed., *N.v.B.* (Coburg, 1947).

Grolmann, Adolf von, ed., *Die Nachtwachen des Bonaventura* (Heidelberg, 1955).

Riemeck, Renate, ed., *N.v.B.* (Frechen-Cologne, 1955).

Hofmann, Annemarie, ed., *N.v.B.* (= *Die Perlenkette*, No. 42) (Stuttgart, 1960).

Müller, Helmut, ed., *Die Nachtwachen des Bonaventura* (= *Goldmanns Liebhaberausgaben*, special edition of the following item) (Munich, 1960).

Müller, Helmut, ed., *Die Nachtwachen des Bonaventura* (= *Goldmanns gelbe Taschenbücher*, No. 627) (Munich, 1960).

Martini, Fritz, ed., *N.v.B.* (= *Klassische Deutsche Dichtung in 20 Bänden*, III) (Freiburg, Basel, and Vienna, 1963), 473-592.

Paulsen, Wolfgang, ed., *N.v.B.* (= *Reclams Universal-Bibliothek*, No. 8926/27) (Stuttgart, 1964).

II. SECONDARY MATERIALS DIRECTLY PERTINENT TO THE *NACHTWACHEN*

Beckers, Hubert, *Schelling's Geistesentwicklung in ihrem innern Zusammenhang. Festschrift zu Friedrich Wilhelm Joseph Schelling's hundertjährigem Geburtstag* (Munich, 1875).

Berend, Eduard, "Der Typus des Humoristen", *Die Ernte* [Festschrift for Franz Muncker] (Halle, 1926).

——, "Zu den Nachtwachen von Bonaventura", *Zeitschrift für deutsche Philologie*, LI (1926), 329-330.

Bonaventura, [pseud.], "Des Teufels Taschenbuch. Einleitung", *Zeitung für die elegante Welt,* March 26, 1805 (No. 37), cols. 294-296.
This advertisement, clearly by the same hand as the *Nachtwachen,* promised, in a footnote signed "Bonaventura", the entire work for Easter, 1805; it seems never to have appeared. The passage is reprinted in Erich Frank's edition of 1912, pp. 167-168. A further advertisement, which speaks of "ein *Pendant von den Nachtwachen von Bonaventura von demselben Verfasser*", appeared in another of Dienemann's journals, *Konstantinopel und St. Petersburg. Der Orient und der Norden. Eine Zeitschrift herausgegeben von H. von Reimers und F. Murhard,* Vol. I (1805). The text is given by E. Schulte-Strathaus, "Nachrichten", *Euphorion,* XIV (1907), 823.

Deibel, Franz, "Ein romantisches Kaleidoskop", *Freistatt,* VII (1905).
Unavailable to me. It may be the same article as the following item.

——, "Ein romantisches Kaleidoskop", *Die Gegenwart,* LXXVII (1910), 109-111.

Eckertz, Erich, "Nachtwachen von Bonaventura. Ein Spiel mit Schelling und Goethe gegen die Schlegels und Caroline", *Zeitschrift für Bücherfreunde,* IX (1905-06), 234-249.

Frank, Erich, "Clemens Brentano, Nachtwachen von Bonaventura", *Germanisch-Romanische Monatsschrift,* IV (1912), 417-440. See also Frank's edition of 1912.

Gölz, Sigrid, "Die Formen der Unmittelbarkeit in den Nachtwachen von Bonaventura" (Diss. Frankfurt am Main, [1955]).

Gundolf, Friedrich, "Über Clemens Brentano", *Zeitschrift für Deutschkunde,* XLII (1928), 1-17; 97-115. See also under Schultz, Franz.

Haller, Rudolf, *Die Romantik in der Zeit der Umkehr* (Bonn, 1941).

Hase, Karl von, *Ideale und Irrtümer* (Leipzig, 1873).

Haym, Rudolf, *Die romantische Schule* (Berlin, 1870).

Hofmann, Karl, "Zur Verfasserfrage der Nachtwachen von Bonaventura" (Diss. Prague, [1921]).

Jean Paul, *Denkwürdigkeiten aus dem Leben von Jean Paul Friedrich Richter,* ed. Ernst Förster (Munich, 1863).

Kayser, Wolfgang, *Das Groteske in Malerei und Dichtung* (Oldenburg, 1957).

Körner, Josef, *August Wilhelm und Friedrich Schlegel im Briefwechsel mit Schiller und Goethe* (Leipzig, 1926).

———, *Sub* "Bonaventura", *Der Große Brockhaus,* 15th edn., III (Leipzig, 1929), 144; *sub* "Fischer, Johann Karl Christian", *ibid.,* VI (Leipzig, 1930), 268.

Köster, Heinrich, "Das Phänomen des Lächerlichen in der Dichtung um 1800 (Jean Paul, E. T. A. Hoffmann, Bonaventura)" (Diss. Freiburg im Breisgau, [1956]).

Kohlschmidt, Werner, "Das Hamlet-Motiv in den 'Nachtwachen' des Bonaventura", *German Studies Presented to Walter Horace Bruford* (London, 1962).

———, "Nihilismus der Romantik", *Neue schweizer Rundschau,* XXI (Dec., 1953), 466-482. Reprinted in: *Form und Innerlichkeit* (Bern, 1955).

Korff, H. A., *Geist der Goethezeit,* Vol. III: *Frühromantik* (Leipzig, 1949).

Majut, Richard, *Lebensbühne und Marionette. Ein Beitrag zur seelengeschichtlichen Entwicklung von der Genie-Zeit bis zum Biedermeier* (= *Germanische Studien,* No. 100) (Berlin, 1931).

Meissner, Alfred, *Mosaik* (Berlin, 1886). *Nachtwachen* materials reprinted from unidentified article. See Schultz, *Verfasser,* p. 60.

Meyer, Hermann, *Der Typus des Sonderlings in der deutschen Literatur* (Amsterdam, 1943).

Meyer, Richard M., "Nachtwachen von Bonaventura", *Euphorion,* X (1903), 578-588.

Michel, Hermann, "Nachtwachen von Bonaventura", *Nationalzeitung,* Jan. 13, 15, 1904. The materials in this article were incorporated in the apparatus to his edition of 1904.

Müller, Joachim, "Die Nachtwachen von Bonaventura", *Neue Jahrbücher für Wissenschaft und Jugendbildung,* XII (1936), 433-444.

Nadler, Josef, *Literaturgeschichte der deutschen Stämme und Landschaften*, Vol. III, 2nd edn. (Regensburg, 1924).

Naumann, Hans, "Zu den Nachtwachen von Bonaventura", *Zeitschrift für deutsche Philologie*, XLIX (1923), 240-243.

Obenauer, K. J., *Die Problematik des ästhetischen Menschen in der deutschen Literatur* (Munich, 1933).

Ranke, Friedrich, "Mitteilungen über F. G. Wetzel", *Euphorion*, XVIII (1911), 741-746.

Rapp, Eleonore, *Die Marionette in der deutschen Dichtung von Sturm und Drang bis zur Romantik* (Leipzig, 1924).

Rassmann, Christian Friedrich, *Gallerie der jetzt lebenden deutschen Dichter, Romanschriftsteller, Erzähler, Übersetzer aus neueren Sprachen, Anthologen und Herausgeber*, 2nd edn. (Helmstädt, 1818).

——, *Kurzgefaßtes Lexikon deutscher pseudonymer Schriftsteller von der ältern bis auf die jüngste Zeit* (Leipzig, 1830).

Rehm, Walter, *Reallexikon der deutschen Literaturgeschichte*, ed. P. Merker and W. Stammler, *sub* "Satirischer Roman" (Berlin, 1928-29).

Ryssel, F. H., "F. G. Wetzel innerhalb der geistigen und politischen Erneuerung im Zeitalter der Romantik" (Diss. Frankfurt am Main, 1939).

Sammons, Jeffrey L., "A Structural Analysis of the Nachtwachen von Bonaventura" (Diss. New Haven, Connecticut, 1962).

Schmidt, Erich, "Nachtwachen von Bonaventura", *Vierteljahrschrift für Literaturgeschichte*, I (1888), 502.

Schulte-Strathaus, E., "Nachrichten", *Euphorion*, XIV (1907), 823.

Schultz, Franz, "Bibliographisches Repertorium", *Euphorion*, XIV (1907), 399.

——, "Gundolf und die Nachtwachen von Bonaventura", *Euphorion*, XXIX (1928), 234-239.
See also under Gundolf, Friedrich.

——, *Der Verfasser der Nachtwachen von Bonaventura. Untersuchungen zur deutschen Romantik* (Berlin, 1909).
Reviews: Berend, Eduard, *Literaturblatt für germanische und romanische Philologie*, XXXII (1911), cols. 229-232. – Kosch, Wilhelm, *Literarische Rundschau für das katholische Deutschland*, XXXVII (1911), cols. 502-504. – Meyer, Richard M., *Euphorion*, XVI (1909), 797-800. – Schulze, Friedrich, *Literarisches Zentralblatt*, LXI (1910), cols. 690-691.
See also Schultz's editions of 1909, 1919, and 1947, and his review of Frank's edition of 1912.

Seydel, Rudolf, "Schellings Nachtwachen", *Zeitschrift für deutsches Altertum*, XXIII (1879), 203-205.

[Sölle]-Nipperdey, Dorothee, "Untersuchungen zur Struktur der Nachtwachen von Bonaventura" (Diss. Göttingen, 1954).

Sölle-Nipperdey, Dorothee, *Untersuchungen zur Struktur der Nachtwachen von Bonaventura* (= *Palaestra*, No. 230) (Göttingen, 1959).

Stachow, Joachim, "Studien zu den Nachtwachen von Bonaventura mit besonderer Berücksichtigung des Marionettenproblems" (Diss. Hamburg, [1957]).

Steig, Reinhold, "Friedrich Gottlob Wetzel als Beiträger zu Heinrich von Kleists Berliner Abendblättern. Zu Kleists hundertjährigem Todestage", *Archiv für das Studium der neueren Sprachen und Literaturen*, CXXVII (1911), 25-30.

Thiele, J., "Untersuchungen zur Frage des Autors der 'Nachtwachen von Bonaventura' mit Hilfe einfacher Textcharakteristiken", *Grundlagenstudien aus Kybernetik und Geisteswissenschaft*, IV (1963), 36-44.

Thimme, Gottfried, "Nachtwachen von Bonaventura", *Euphorion*, XIII (1906), 159-184.

Trube, Hans, *Friedrich Gottlob Wetzels Leben und Werk mit besonderer Berücksichtigung seiner Lyrik* (= *Germanische Studien*, No. 58). (Berlin, 1928).

Review: Berend, Eduard, *Deutsche Literaturzeitung*, n.s. VI (1929), cols. 861-864.

Varnhagen von Ense, Karl August, *Tagebücher* (Leipzig, 1861-70).

III. OTHER MATERIALS CONSULTED FOR THIS STUDY

Appell, J. W., *Die Ritter-, Räuber-, und Schauerromantik. Zur Geschichte der deutschen Unterhaltungs-Literatur* (Leipzig, 1859).

Arnim, Hans von, *Sprachliche Forschungen zur Chronologie der Platonischen Dialoge* (= *Sitzungsberichte der Kaiserlichen Akademie der Wissenschaften in Wien*, Philosophische-Historische Klasse, CLXIX, Abhandlung 3) (Vienna, 1912).

Bauer, Rudolf, *Der historische Trivialroman in Deutschland im ausgehenden 18. Jahrhundert* (Plauen, 1930).

Brentano, Clemens, *Sämtliche Werke*, ed. Carl Schüddekopf, et al., Vol. V (Munich and Leipzig, 1909).

Dieckmann, Lieselotte, "The Metaphor of Hieroglyphics in German Romanticism", *Comparative Literature*, VII (1955), 306-312.

Funck, Z., [pseud.]. See Kunz, Karl Friedrich.

Gassen, Kurt, *Die Chronologie der Novellen Heinrich von Kleists* (= *Forschungen zur neueren Literaturgeschichte*, Vol. LV) (Weimar, 1920).

Goethe, Johann Wolfgang von, *Werke*, ed. Erich Trunz, et al. (Hamburg, 1948-60).

Grimm, Jakob and Wilhelm, *Deutsches Wörterbuch*, Vol. V. (Leipzig, 1873).

Gundolf, Friedrich, *Romantiker* (Berlin, 1930).

Heine, Heinrich, *Sämtliche Werke*, ed. Ernst Elster (Leipzig and Vienna, [1887-90]).

Huch, Ricarda, *Die Romantik*, Vol. I: *Blütezeit der Romantik* (Leipzig, 1931).

Jean Paul, *Sämmtliche Werke*, ed. Ernst Förster, 3rd edn. (Berlin, 1860-62).

——, *Werke*, ed. Gustav Lohmann, Norbert Miller, et al. (Munich, 1959-).

Klinger, Friedrich Maximilian, *Fausts Leben, Thaten und Höllenfahrt*, 2d edn. (Karlsruhe, 1792).

Körner, Josef, "Die Wiener 'Friedensblätter' 1814-15, eine romantische Zeitschrift", *Zeitschrift für Bücherfreunde*, n.s. XIV (1912), 90-98.

[Kunz, Karl Friedrich], *Erinnerungen aus meinem Leben in biographischen Denksteinen und anderen Mittheilungen*, Vol. I: *Aus dem Leben zweier Dichter: Ernst Theodor Wilhelm Hoffmann's und Friedrich Gottlob Wetzel's* (Leipzig, 1836).

Liepe, Wolfgang, "Hebbel und Schelling", *Deutsche Beiträge*, ed. Arnold Bergsträsser (Chicago and Munich, 1953), pp. 121-181.

Mack, Sidney F., *Elementary Statistics* (New York, 1960).

Martini, Fritz, *Deutsche Literaturgeschichte von den Anfängen bis zur Gegenwart*, 7th edn. (Stuttgart, 1956).

Moritz, Karl Philipp, *Anton Reiser*, ed. Max von Brück (Leipzig, n.d.).

Morris, Max, *Goethes und Herders Anteil an dem Jahrgang 1772 der Frankfurter gelehrten Anzeigen* (Stuttgart, 1909).

Nicolai, Karl, *Franz von Werden* (Penig, 1802).

Novalis, *Schriften*, ed. J. Minor (Jena, 1907).

Nutz, Walter, *Der Trivialroman. Seine Formen und seine Hersteller. Ein Beitrag zur Literatursoziologie* (Cologne and Opladen, 1962).

Rasch, Wolfdietrich, "Die Zeit der Klassik und frühen Romantik", *Annalen der deutschen Literatur*, ed. H. O. Burger (Stuttgart, 1952).

Rehm, Walter, *Experimentum mediatis* (Munich, 1947).

Ritter, Constantin, "Anwendung der Sprach-Stilistik auf die Recensionen in den Frankfurter gelehrten Anzeigen von 1772", *Goethe-Jahrbuch*, XXIV (1903), 185-203.

——, "Die Sprachstatistik in Anwendung auf Goethes Prosa", *Euphorion*, X (1903), 558-578.

——, "Die Sprachstatistik in Anwendung auf Platon und Goethe", *Neue Jahrbücher für das klassische Altertum Geschichte und deutsche Literatur*, XI (1903), 241-261, 313-325.

Schiller, Friedrich, *Sämtliche Werke*, ed. Gerhard Fricke und Herbert G. Göpfert (Munich, 1958-59).

Schubert, Gotthilf Heinrich, *Der Erwerb aus einem vergangenen und die Erwartungen von einem zukünftigen Leben* (Erlangen, 1854-56).

Thalmann, Marianne, *Der Trivialroman des 18. Jahrhunderts und der romantische Roman* (Berlin, 1923).

Thompson, Stith, *Motif-Index of Folk-Literature*, 2d edn. (Bloomington, Indiana, 1955-58).

Tieck, Ludwig, *Schriften* (Berlin, 1828).

Traversi, D. A., *An Approach to Shakespeare*, 2d edn. (Garden City, New York, 1956).

[Vulpius, Christian], *Don Juan der Wüstling. Nach dem Spanischen des Tirso de Molina* (Penig, 1805).

Wetzel, Friedrich Gottlob, *Einige Briefe von Friedrich Gottlob Wetzel, herausgegeben und seinem Töchterchen Minna zum Tauftage gewidmet von Friedrich Engel* (Leipzig, 1903).

——, *F. G. Wetzel's gesammelte Gedichte und Nachlaß*, ed. Z. Funck [Karl Friedrich Kunz] (Leipzig, 1838).

——, *Hermannfried letzter König von Thüringien* (Berlin, 1818).

——, *Magischer Spiegel,* ed. Kristian Kraus (Leipzig, 1939).

——, *Schriftproben von F. G. Wetzel. Mythen – Romanzen – Lyrische Gedichte* (Bamberg, 1814).

——, *Schriftproben von F. C.* [sic] *Wetzel. Zweytes Bändchen* (Bamberg and Leipzig, 1818).